# Affordable and Essential UK Air Fryer

## Cookbook for Beginners 2023

**1000** Days of Delicious and Easy Air Fryer Recipes with Simple-to-Follow Instructions for Home Cooking

*Neoma Fritsch*

# Table of Contents

INTRODUCTION ............................................................. 1

Air Fryer Basics ................................................. 2
Benefits of Air Frying.......................................... 3
How to Choose the Air Fryer That Suits You?......................4

Air Fryer Maintenance Tips ...................................5
Start Air Frying Now............................................6

## Chapter 1 Breakfasts .................................... 7

Chimichanga Breakfast Burrito...................................8
Butternut Squash and Ricotta Frittata .........................8
Gold Avocado...................................................8
Cauliflower Avocado Toast .....................................8
Portobello Eggs Benedict.......................................9
Hearty Cheddar Biscuits .......................................9
Golden Avocado Tempura ........................................9
Oat Bran Muffins...............................................9
Sausage and Cheese Balls .....................................10
Parmesan Sausage Egg Muffins .................................10
Mexican Breakfast Pepper Rings ...............................10
Strawberry Tarts .............................................10
Bacon, Cheese, and Avocado Melt...............................10

Bourbon Vanilla French Toast..................................11
Easy Sausage Pizza ...........................................11
Poached Eggs on Whole Grain Avocado Toast ....................11
Breakfast Calzone ............................................11
Oat and Chia Porridge ........................................11
Cinnamon Rolls................................................12
Spinach and Swiss Frittata with Mushrooms ....................12
Cajun Breakfast Sausage.......................................12
French Toast Sticks ..........................................12
Simple Scotch Eggs............................................13
Green Eggs and Ham ...........................................13
Broccoli-Mushroom Frittata....................................13

## Chapter 2 Family Favorites .......................... 14

Bacon-Wrapped Hot Dogs .......................................15
Coconut Chicken Tenders ......................................15
Berry Cheesecake .............................................15
Steak and Vegetable Kebabs ...................................15
Beignets......................................................16

Mixed Berry Crumble ..........................................16
Filo Vegetable Triangles......................................16
Fish and Vegetable Tacos .....................................16
Meringue Cookies .............................................17
Steak Tips and Potatoes.......................................17

## Chapter 3 Fast and Easy Everyday Favourites ............ 18

Sweet Corn and Carrot Fritters ...............................19
Simple Pea Delight............................................19
Crunchy Fried Okra............................................19
Air Fried Shishito Peppers ...................................19
Rosemary and Orange Roasted Chickpeas ........................20
Herb-Roasted Veggies..........................................20
Simple and Easy Croutons .....................................20
Baked Halloumi with Greek Salsa ..............................20
Air Fried Courgette Sticks....................................20

Cheesy Chilli Toast ..........................................21
Buttery Sweet Potatoes .......................................21
Traditional Queso Fundido.....................................21
Baked Chorizo Scotch Eggs ....................................21
Easy Devils on Horseback .....................................21
Bacon Pinwheels...............................................22

## Chapter 4 Poultry

23

Cornish Hens with Honey-Lime Glaze ...24
Korean Honey Wings ...24
Bacon Lovers' Stuffed Chicken ...24
Chicken Shawarma ...25
Fried Chicken Breasts ...25
Pecan Turkey Cutlets ...25
Herbed Roast Chicken Breast ...25
Chicken Pesto Parmigiana ...26
Chicken, Courgette, and Spinach Salad ...26
Garlic Dill Wings ...26
Ham Chicken with Cheese ...26
Chicken Wings with Piri Piri Sauce ...27
Coconut Chicken Wings with Mango Sauce ...27

Israeli Chicken Schnitzel ...27
Yellow Curry Chicken Thighs with Peanuts ...28
Chicken Rochambeau ...28
Ginger Turmeric Chicken Thighs ...28
Blackened Chicken ...28
Cheesy Pepperoni and Chicken Pizza ...29
Greek Chicken Stir-Fry ...29
Potato-Crusted Chicken ...29
Crunchy Chicken Tenders ...29
Smoky Chicken Leg Quarters ...29
Brazilian Tempero Baiano Chicken Drumsticks ...30
Cranberry Curry Chicken ...30

## Chapter 5 Beef, Pork, and Lamb
31

Simple Beef Mince with Courgette ...32
Barbecue Ribs ...32
Garlic Butter Steak Bites ...32
Chorizo and Beef Burger ...32
Greek Stuffed Fillet ...33
Chuck Kebab with Rocket ...33
Goat Cheese-Stuffed Bavette Steak ...33
Mojito Lamb Chops ...33
Ham Hock Mac and Cheese ...34
Parmesan-Crusted Steak ...34
Pork Loin with Aloha Salsa ...34
Indian Mint and Chile Kebabs ...34
Italian Pork Loin ...35

Steak with Bell Pepper ...35
Rosemary Roast Beef ...35
Asian Glazed Meatballs ...35
BBQ Pork Steaks ...36
Pork Medallions with Endive Salad ...36
Pork Chops with Caramelized Onions ...36
Mexican Pork Chops ...36
Italian Sausage Links ...37
Rack of Lamb with Pistachio Crust ...37
Marinated Steak Tips with Mushrooms ...37
Honey-Baked Pork Loin ...37
Pork Tenderloin with Avocado Lime Sauce ...38

## Chapter 6 Fish and Seafood
39

Crab Legs ...40
Crab Cakes with Mango Mayo ...40
Sole Fillets ...40
Simple Buttery Cod ...40
Breaded Prawns Tacos ...41
Trout Amandine with Lemon Butter Sauce ...41
Almond Pesto Salmon ...41
Almond-Crusted Fish ...41
Tilapia Sandwiches with Tartar Sauce ...42
Honey-Balsamic Salmon ...42
Seasoned Tuna Steaks ...42
Mouthwatering Cod over Creamy Leek Noodles ...42
Baked Tilapia with Garlic Aioli ...43
Tandoori Prawns ...43

Easy Scallops ...43
Nutty Prawns with Amaretto Glaze ...43
chilli Lime Prawns ...44
Sweet Tilapia Fillets ...44
Greek Fish Pitas ...44
Browned Prawns Patties ...44
Parmesan-Crusted Hake with Garlic Sauce ...44
Tuna Patty Sliders ...45
Prawns Scampi ...45
Tuna Melt ...45
Cajun and Lemon Pepper Cod ...45

# Chapter 7 Snacks and Appetizers

Crispy Filo Artichoke Triangles ......................... 47
Classic Spring Rolls ....................................... 47
Bacon-Wrapped A Pickled Gherkin Spear ........... 47
Jalapeño Poppers .......................................... 48
Five-Ingredient Falafel with Garlic-Yoghurt Sauce ... 48
Crispy Green Bean Fries with Lemon-Yoghurt Sauce ... 48
Browned Ricotta with Capers and Lemon ............ 48
String Bean Fries ........................................... 49
Sweet Bacon Potato Crunchies ......................... 49
Old Bay Chicken Wings ................................... 49
Air Fried Pot Stickers ..................................... 49
Ranch Oyster Snack Crackers .......................... 49
Tangy Fried A Pickle Gherkin Spears ................ 50

Crispy Mozzarella Cheese Sticks ...................... 50
Mixed Vegetables Pot Stickers ......................... 50
Lemon Prawns with Garlic Olive Oil ................. 50
Cheese Drops .............................................. 51
Hush Puppies .............................................. 51
Kale Chips with Tex-Mex Dip .......................... 51
Pepperoni Pizza Dip ...................................... 51
Garlic-Roasted Tomatoes and Olives ................ 52
Bruschetta with Basil Pesto ............................ 52
Pickle Chips ................................................ 52
Stuffed Figs with Goat Cheese and Honey ......... 52
Artichoke and Olive Pitta Flatbread .................. 52

# Chapter 8 Vegetables and Sides

Crispy Chickpeas .......................................... 54
Caesar Whole Cauliflower ............................... 54
Sesame Carrots and Sugar Snap Peas ................ 54
Rosemary-Roasted Red Potatoes ...................... 54
Garlic-Parmesan Crispy Baby Potatoes .............. 55
Stuffed Red Peppers with Herbed Ricotta and Tomatoes.......... 55
Breaded Green Tomatoes ................................. 55
Sausage-Stuffed Mushroom Caps ..................... 55
Zesty Fried Asparagus .................................... 56
Garlic and Thyme Tomatoes ............................ 56
Cauliflower Rice Balls .................................... 56
Roasted Radishes with Sea Salt ....................... 56
Parmesan Herb Focaccia Bread ........................ 56

Garlic Herb Radishes ..................................... 57
Parmesan-Rosemary Radishes ......................... 57
Caramelized Aubergine with Harissa Yogurt ...... 57
Hawaiian Brown Rice ..................................... 57
Broccoli-Cheddar Twice-Baked Potatoes ........... 57
Brussels Sprouts with Pecans and Gorgonzola ... 58
Green Peas with Mint ..................................... 58
Crispy Lemon Artichoke Hearts ....................... 58
Chiles Rellenos with Red Chile Sauce ............... 58
Buttery Green Beans ...................................... 59
Roasted Salsa .............................................. 59
Buttery Mushrooms ....................................... 59

# Chapter 9 Vegetarian Mains

Crispy Cabbage Steaks .................................... 61
Spaghetti Squash Alfredo ................................ 61
Super Vegetable Burger ................................... 61
Roasted Vegetable Mélange with Herbs .............. 61
Spinach-Artichoke Stuffed Mushrooms .............. 62

Aubergine Parmesan ...................................... 62
Pesto Spinach Flatbread .................................. 62
Herbed Broccoli with Cheese ........................... 62
Courgette-Ricotta Tart .................................... 63
Super Veg Rolls ............................................ 63

# Chapter 10 Desserts

Cream Cheese Danish ..................................... 65
Brown Sugar Banana Bread .............................. 65
Coconut-Custard Pie ...................................... 65
Gingerbread ................................................ 65
Blackberry Cobbler ....................................... 66
Pumpkin Spice Pecans ................................... 66
Applesauce and Chocolate Brownies ................. 66
Lemon Curd Pavlova ...................................... 66
Coconut Mixed Berry Crisp ............................. 67

Baked Brazilian Pineapple ............................... 67
Peaches and Apple Crumble ............................ 67
Pears with Honey-Lemon Ricotta ..................... 67
Peanut Butter, Honey & Banana Toast ............... 67
Cherry Pie .................................................. 68
Grilled Peaches ............................................ 68

# INTRODUCTION

Air fryers have become a must-have kitchen appliance, offering a healthier and more convenient alternative to traditional frying methods. With this cookbook, you will discover how to make delicious and nutritious meals that are easy to prepare and packed with flavor.

The UK food culture is diverse and vibrant, and this cookbook celebrates this diversity by bringing together a collection of recipes that represent the best of British cuisine. From classic fish and chips to mouth-watering curries, hearty stews, and delectable desserts, you will find something to suit every taste and occasion.

But this cookbook is not just about recipes. I will also share my expertise on how to use your air fryer effectively, providing tips on how to achieve the perfect temperature, texture, and flavor. You will learn how to make the most of your air fryer, whether you are cooking for one or for a crowd.

With this cookbook, you can say goodbye to greasy, unhealthy meals and hello to flavorful, nutritious dishes that are easy to prepare and a joy to eat. So, get ready to unleash the full potential of your air fryer and take your cooking to the next level. I can't wait for you to try out these recipes and experience the joy of cooking with an air fryer.

# Air Fryer Basics

When it comes to cooking, the air fryer has become a staple in many British kitchens. But what exactly is an air fryer, and how does it work?

At its core, an air fryer is a kitchen appliance that uses hot air to cook food. It's a healthier alternative to traditional frying methods, as it requires little to no oil. The hot air circulates around the food, cooking it evenly and quickly.

To use an air fryer, you first need to preheat it to the desired temperature. Most air fryers come with temperature settings that range from 180°C to 200°C. Once preheated, you can place the food in the basket and set the timer. Cooking times vary depending on the recipe, but most dishes can be cooked in 10-20 minutes.

One of the benefits of using an air fryer is that it can cook a wide variety of foods, from frozen foods to fresh vegetables and even baked goods. It's a versatile appliance that can help you create healthy and delicious meals with ease.

However, it's important to note that not all air fryers are created equal. Different models may have different features and cooking capacities, so it's essential to choose the right one for your needs. It's also crucial to read the manufacturer's instructions carefully to ensure safe and effective use of the appliance.

The air fryer is a valuable tool for any British cook looking to create healthy and delicious meals. By understanding the basics of how it works and choosing the right model for your needs, you can take advantage of this versatile kitchen appliance to create a variety of tasty dishes with ease.

## Benefits of Air Frying

Air frying has gained popularity in recent years as a healthier alternative to traditional frying methods. But what are the actual benefits of air frying, and why should you consider using this method in your cooking?

Firstly, air frying uses significantly less oil than traditional frying methods, which can result in healthier and lower calorie meals. This is particularly important for those who are watching their weight or looking to improve their overall health.

Secondly, air frying can save you time and effort in the kitchen. Unlike traditional frying methods, there is no need for messy and time-consuming cleanup. Additionally, air frying can cook food quickly and evenly, allowing you to prepare meals faster and with less effort.

Thirdly, air frying can be a versatile method of cooking, allowing you to cook a wide range of foods with ease. From crispy chicken wings to roasted vegetables, the air fryer can handle a variety of dishes, making it a valuable addition to any kitchen.

Finally, air frying can be an environmentally-friendly cooking method. As it uses less oil, there is less waste to dispose of, and the appliance itself consumes less energy than traditional ovens or deep fryers.

Air frying offers a range of benefits that make it a valuable cooking method for any health-conscious, time-strapped, and environmentally-aware British cook. By incorporating air frying into your cooking routine, you can create delicious and healthy meals while saving time and effort in the kitchen.

## How to Choose the Air Fryer That Suits You?

Choosing the right air fryer for your needs can be a daunting task, given the wide variety of models and features available on the market. However, with a bit of research and careful consideration, you can find the air fryer that suits you best.

Firstly, consider the size of the air fryer. If you have a large family or entertain frequently, you may want to opt for a larger model that can cook larger quantities of food at once. However, if you have limited counter space, a smaller model may be a better fit.

Secondly, consider the wattage of the air fryer. Higher wattage can mean faster and more efficient cooking, but it also means higher energy consumption. Think about your priorities in terms of cooking speed versus energy efficiency when making your decision.

Thirdly, consider the features of the air fryer. Do you need a model with multiple cooking functions, such as baking or grilling? Do you prefer a digital or manual control panel? Do you need an air fryer with a built-in timer or a delay start function? Consider your cooking needs and preferences when choosing the features that matter most to you.

Fourthly, read reviews and do research on the brand and model you are considering. Look for user reviews that highlight the pros and cons of each model, as well as any common issues or complaints. This can give you a better idea of what to expect from your air fryer and help you make an informed decision.

Choosing the right air fryer requires careful consideration of factors such as size, wattage, features, and brand reputation. By taking the time to research and evaluate different models, you can find the air fryer that best suits your cooking needs and preferences.

## Air Fryer Maintenance Tips

Proper maintenance is essential to keep your air fryer working efficiently and effectively over time. Here are some tips to help you maintain your air fryer in good condition:

1.Clean your air fryer after each use. This will prevent the buildup of grease and food particles that can affect the performance of your appliance. Use a damp cloth or sponge to wipe down the interior and exterior of the air fryer, and remove any excess oil from the basket and tray.

2.Check the heating element and fan regularly. Over time, the heating element and fan may become clogged with grease or food particles. Check these components regularly to ensure that they are free of debris and working effectively.

3.Avoid using harsh or abrasive cleaning products. Chemicals or abrasive cleaning products can damage the surface of your air fryer. Stick to mild soap and water when cleaning your appliance, and avoid using steel wool or other abrasive materials.

4.Use a non-stick spray or parchment paper to prevent food from sticking to the basket. This will make cleaning your air fryer easier and prevent food from burning or sticking to the basket.

5.Store your air fryer in a clean, dry place. When not in use, store your air fryer in a cool, dry place, away from direct sunlight or heat sources.

6.By following these simple maintenance tips, you can keep your air fryer in good condition and ensure that it continues to provide delicious and healthy meals for years to come.

## Start Air Frying Now

Not only does air frying result in healthier, lower-calorie meals, it's also a versatile and time-saving cooking method that can handle a wide range of dishes. Whether you're cooking chicken wings, roasted vegetables, or even desserts, the air fryer can handle it all.

Plus, with a variety of models and features to choose from, there's an air fryer out there for every kitchen and every cook. Whether you're a beginner or a seasoned chef, air frying can be a valuable addition to your cooking routine.

So why not give air frying another try? With its many benefits and delicious results, it's a cooking method that's definitely worth exploring. Who knows - you might just be surprised at how much you enjoy it!

# Chapter 1 Breakfasts

# Chapter 1 Breakfasts

## Chimichanga Breakfast Burrito

**Prep time: 10 minutes | Cook time: 10 minutes | Serves 2**

2 large (10- to 12-inch) wheat tortillas
120 g canned refried beans (pinto or black work equally well)
4 large eggs, cooked scrambled
4 corn tortilla chips, crushed
120 g grated chili cheese
12 pickled jalapeño slices
1 tablespoon vegetable oil
Guacamole, tomato salsa, and sour cream, for serving (optional)

1. Place the tortillas on a work surface and divide the refried beans between them, spreading them in a rough rectangle in the center of the tortillas. Top the beans with the scrambled eggs, crushed chips, cheese, and jalapeños. Fold one side over the fillings, then fold in each short side and roll up the rest of the way like a burrito. 2. Brush the outside of the burritos with the oil, then transfer to the air fryer, seam-side down. Air fry at 180ºC until the tortillas are browned and crisp and the filling is warm throughout, about 10 minutes. 3. Transfer the chimichangas to plates and serve warm with guacamole, tomato salsa, and sour cream, if you like.

## Butternut Squash and Ricotta Frittata

**Prep time: 10 minutes | Cook time: 33 minutes | Serves 2 to 3**

235 ml cubed (½-inch) butternut squash (160 g)
2 tablespoons rapeseed oil
Coarse or flaky salt and freshly ground black pepper, to taste
4 fresh sage leaves, thinly sliced
6 large eggs, lightly beaten
120 g ricotta cheese
Cayenne pepper

1. In a bowl, toss the squash with the rapeseed oil and season with salt and black pepper until evenly coated. Sprinkle the sage on the bottom of a cake pan and place the squash on top. Place the pan in the air fryer and bake at 200ºC for 10 minutes. Stir to incorporate the sage, then cook until the squash is tender and lightly caramelized at the edges, about 3 minutes more. 2. Pour the eggs over the squash, dollop the ricotta all over, and sprinkle with cayenne. Bake at 150ºC until the eggs are set and the frittata is golden brown on top, about 20 minutes. Remove the pan from the air fryer and cut the frittata into wedges to serve.

## Gold Avocado

**Prep time: 5 minutes | Cook time: 6 minutes | Serves 4**

2 large avocados, sliced
¼ teaspoon paprika
Salt and ground black pepper, to taste
60 g flour
2 eggs, beaten
120 g bread crumbs

1. Preheat the air fryer to 200ºC. 2. Sprinkle paprika, salt and pepper on the slices of avocado. 3. Lightly coat the avocados with flour. Dredge them in the eggs, before covering with bread crumbs. 4. Transfer to the air fryer and air fry for 6 minutes. 5. Serve warm.

## Cauliflower Avocado Toast

**Prep time: 15 minutes | Cook time: 8 minutes | Serves 2**

1 (40 g) steamer bag cauliflower
1 large egg
120 g grated Cheddar cheese
1 ripe medium avocado
½ teaspoon garlic powder
¼ teaspoon ground black pepper

1. Cook cauliflower according to package instructions. Remove from bag and place into cheesecloth or clean towel to remove excess moisture. 2. Place cauliflower into a large bowl and mix in egg and Mozzarella. Cut a piece of parchment to fit your air fryer basket. Separate the cauliflower mixture into two, and place it on the parchment in two mounds. Press out the cauliflower mounds into a ¼-inch-thick rectangle. Place the parchment into the air fryer basket. 3. Adjust the temperature to 200ºC and set the timer for 8 minutes. 4. Flip the cauliflower halfway through the cooking time. 5. When the timer beeps, remove the parchment and allow the cauliflower to cool 5 minutes. 6. Cut open the avocado and remove the pit. Scoop out the inside, place it in a medium bowl, and mash it with garlic powder and pepper. Spread onto the cauliflower. Serve immediately.

# Portobello Eggs Benedict

**Prep time: 10 minutes | Cook time: 10 to 14 minutes | Serves 2**

| | |
|---|---|
| 1 tablespoon rapeseed oil | pepper, to taste |
| 2 cloves garlic, minced | 2 large eggs |
| ¼ teaspoon dried thyme | 2 tablespoons grated Pecorino |
| 2 portobello mushrooms, stems removed and gills scraped out | Romano cheese |
| 2 vine tomatoes, halved lengthwise | 1 tablespoon chopped fresh parsley, for garnish |
| Salt and freshly ground black | 1 teaspoon truffle oil (optional) |

1. Preheat the air fryer to 200ºC. 2. In a small bowl, combine the rapeseed oil, garlic, and thyme. Brush the mixture over the mushrooms and tomatoes until thoroughly coated. Season to taste with salt and freshly ground black pepper. 3. Arrange the vegetables, cut side up, in the air fryer basket. Crack an egg into the center of each mushroom and sprinkle with cheese. Air fry for 10 to 14 minutes until the vegetables are tender and the whites are firm. When cool enough to handle, coarsely chop the tomatoes and place on top of the eggs. Scatter parsley on top and drizzle with truffle oil, if desired, just before serving.

# Hearty Cheddar Biscuits

**Prep time: 10 minutes | Cook time: 22 minutes | Makes 8 biscuits**

| | |
|---|---|
| 250 g self-raising flour | plus more to melt on top |
| 2 tablespoons sugar | 315 ml buttermilk |
| 120 g butter, frozen for 15 minutes | 235 g plain flour, for shaping |
| 120 g grated Cheddar cheese, | 1 tablespoon butter, melted |

1. Line a buttered 7-inch metal cake pan with parchment paper or a silicone liner. 2. Combine the flour and sugar in a large mixing bowl. Grate the butter into the flour. Add the grated cheese and stir to coat the cheese and butter with flour. Then add the buttermilk and stir just until you can no longer see streaks of flour. The dough should be quite wet. 3. Spread the plain (not self-raising) flour out on a small cookie sheet. With a spoon, scoop 8 evenly sized balls of dough into the flour, making sure they don't touch each other. With floured hands, coat each dough ball with flour and toss them gently from hand to hand to shake off any excess flour. Put each floured dough ball into the prepared pan, right up next to the other. This will help the biscuits rise, rather than spreading out. 4. Preheat the air fryer to 190ºC. 5. Transfer the cake pan to the basket of the air fryer. Let the ends of the aluminum foil sling hang across the cake pan before returning the basket to the air fryer. 6. Air fry for 20 minutes. Check the biscuits twice to make sure they are not getting too brown on top. If they are, re-arrange the aluminum foil strips to cover any brown parts. After 20 minutes, check the biscuits by inserting a toothpick into the center of the biscuits. It should come out clean. If it needs a little more time, continue to air fry for two extra minutes. Brush the tops of the biscuits with some melted butter and sprinkle a little more grated cheese on top if desired. Pop the basket back into the air fryer for another 2 minutes. 7. Remove the cake pan from the air fryer. Let the biscuits cool for just a minute or two and then turn them out onto a plate and pull apart. Serve immediately.

# Golden Avocado Tempura

**Prep time: 5 minutes | Cook time: 10 minutes | Serves 4**

| | |
|---|---|
| 60 g bread crumbs | and sliced |
| ½ teaspoons salt | Liquid from 1 can white beans |
| 1 Haas avocado, pitted, peeled | |

1. Preheat the air fryer to 180ºC. 2. Mix the bread crumbs and salt in a shallow bowl until well-incorporated. 3. Dip the avocado slices in the bean liquid, then into the bread crumbs. 4. Put the avocados in the air fryer, taking care not to overlap any slices, and air fry for 10 minutes, giving the basket a good shake at the halfway point. 5. Serve immediately.

# Oat Bran Muffins

**Prep time: 10 minutes | Cook time: 10 to 12 minutes per batch | Makes 8 muffins**

| | |
|---|---|
| 160 g oat bran | 120 ml buttermilk |
| 60 g flour | 1 egg |
| 45 g soft brown sugar | 2 tablespoons rapeseed oil |
| 1 teaspoon baking powder | 120 g chopped dates, raisins, or |
| ½ teaspoon baking soda | dried cranberries |
| ⅛ teaspoon salt | 24 paper muffin cases |
| Cooking spray | |

1. Preheat the air fryer to 170ºC. 2. In a large bowl, combine the oat bran, flour, soft brown sugar, baking powder, baking soda, and salt. 3. In a small bowl, beat together the buttermilk, egg, and oil. 4. Pour buttermilk mixture into bowl with dry ingredients and stir just until moistened. Do not beat. 5. Gently stir in dried fruit. 6. Use triple baking cups to help muffins hold shape during baking. Spray them with cooking spray, place 4 sets of cups in air fryer basket at a time, and fill each one ¾ full of batter. 7. Cook for 10 to 12 minutes, until top springs back when lightly touched and toothpick inserted in center comes out clean. 8. Repeat for remaining muffins.

## Sausage and Cheese Balls

**Prep time: 10 minutes | Cook time: 12 minutes |**
**Makes 16 balls**

450 g pork sausage meat, removed from casings
120 g grated Cheddar cheese

30 g full-fat soft cheese, softened
1 large egg

1. Mix all ingredients in a large bowl. Form into sixteen (1-inch) balls. Place the balls into the air fryer basket. 2. Adjust the temperature to 200ºC and air fry for 12 minutes. 3. Shake the basket two or three times during cooking. Sausage balls will be browned on the outside and have an internal temperature of at least 64ºC when completely cooked. 4. Serve warm.

## Parmesan Sausage Egg Muffins

**Prep time: 5 minutes | Cook time: 20 minutes |**
**Serves 4**

170 g Italian-seasoned sausage, sliced
6 eggs
30 ml double cream

Salt and ground black pepper, to taste
85 g Parmesan cheese, grated

1. Preheat the air fryer to 180ºC. Grease a muffin pan. 2. Put the sliced sausage in the muffin pan. 3. Beat the eggs with the cream in a bowl and season with salt and pepper. 4. Pour half of the mixture over the sausages in the pan. 5. Sprinkle with cheese and the remaining egg mixture. 6. Bake in the preheated air fryer for 20 minutes or until set. 7. Serve immediately.

## Mexican Breakfast Pepper Rings

**Prep time: 5 minutes | Cook time: 10 minutes |**
**Serves 4**

rapeseed oil
1 large red, yellow, or orange pepper, cut into four ¾-inch rings

4 eggs
Salt and freshly ground black pepper, to taste
2 teaspoons tomato salsa

1. Preheat the air fryer to 180ºC. Lightly spray a baking pan with rapeseed oil. 2. Place 2 bell pepper rings on the pan. Crack one egg into each bell pepper ring. Season with salt and black pepper. 3. Spoon ½ teaspoon of tomato salsa on top of each egg. 4. Place the pan in the air fryer basket. Air fry until the yolk is slightly runny, 5 to 6 minutes or until the yolk is fully cooked, 8 to 10 minutes. 5. Repeat with the remaining 2 pepper rings. Serve hot.

## Strawberry Tarts

**Prep time: 15 minutes | Cook time: 10 minutes |**
**Serves 6**

2 refrigerated piecrusts
120 g strawberry preserves
1 teaspoon cornflour
Cooking oil spray
120 ml low-fat vanilla yoghurt

30 g soft cheese, at room temperature
3 tablespoons icing sugar
Rainbow sprinkles, for decorating

1. Place the piecrusts on a flat surface. Using a knife or pizza cutter, cut each piecrust into 3 rectangles, for 6 total. Discard any unused dough from the piecrust edges. 2. In a small bowl, stir together the preserves and cornflour. Mix well, ensuring there are no lumps of cornflour remaining. 3. Scoop 1 tablespoon of the strawberry mixture onto the top half of each piece of piecrust. 4. Fold the bottom of each piece up to enclose the filling. Using the back of a fork, press along the edges of each tart to seal. 5. Insert the crisper plate into the basket and the basket into the unit. Preheat the unit by selecting BAKE, setting the temperature to 190ºC, and setting the time to 3 minutes. Select START/STOP to begin. 6. Once the unit is preheated, spray the crisper plate with cooking oil. Working in batches, spray the breakfast tarts with cooking oil and place them into the basket in a single layer. Do not stack the tarts. 7. Select BAKE, set the temperature to 190ºC, and set the time to 10 minutes. Select START/STOP to begin. 8. When the cooking is complete, the tarts should be light golden brown. Let the breakfast tarts cool fully before removing them from the basket. 9. Repeat steps 5, 6, 7, and 8 for the remaining breakfast tarts. 10. In a small bowl, stir together the yoghurt, soft cheese, and icing sugar. Spread the breakfast tarts with the frosting and top with sprinkles.

## Bacon, Cheese, and Avocado Melt

**Prep time: 5 minutes | Cook time: 3 to 5 minutes |**
**Serves 2**

1 avocado
4 slices cooked bacon, chopped
2 tablespoons tomato salsa

1 tablespoon double cream
60 g grated Cheddar cheese

1. Preheat the air fryer to 200ºC. 2. Slice the avocado in half lengthwise and remove the stone. To ensure the avocado halves do not roll in the basket, slice a thin piece of skin off the base. 3. In a small bowl, combine the bacon, tomato salsa, and cream. Divide the mixture between the avocado halves and top with the cheese. 4. Place the avocado halves in the air fryer basket and air fry for 3 to 5 minutes until the cheese has melted and begins to brown. Serve warm.

# Bourbon Vanilla French Toast

| | |
|---|---|
| 2 large eggs | 2 tablespoons bourbon |
| 2 tablespoons water | 1 teaspoon vanilla extract |
| 160 ml whole or semi-skimmed milk | 8 (1-inch-thick) French bread slices |
| 1 tablespoon butter, melted | Cooking spray |

1. Preheat the air fryer to 160°C. Line the air fryer basket with parchment paper and spray it with cooking spray. 2. Beat the eggs with the water in a shallow bowl until combined. Add the milk, melted butter, bourbon, and vanilla and stir to mix well. 3. Dredge 4 slices of bread in the batter, turning to coat both sides evenly. Transfer the bread slices onto the parchment paper. 4. Bake for 6 minutes until nicely browned. Flip the slices halfway through the cooking time. 5. Remove from the basket to a plate and repeat with the remaining 4 slices of bread. 6. Serve warm.

# Easy Sausage Pizza

| | |
|---|---|
| 2 tablespoons ketchup | 230 g Cheddar cheese |
| 1 pitta bread | 1 teaspoon garlic powder |
| 80 g sausage meat | 1 tablespoon rapeseed oil |

1. Preheat the air fryer to 170°C. 2. Spread the ketchup over the pitta bread. 3. Top with the sausage meat and cheese. Sprinkle with the garlic powder and rapeseed oil. 4. Put the pizza in the air fryer basket and bake for 6 minutes. 5. Serve warm.

# Poached Eggs on Whole Grain Avocado Toast

| | |
|---|---|
| rapeseed oil cooking spray | 4 pieces wholegrain bread |
| 4 large eggs | 1 avocado |
| Salt | Red pepper flakes (optional) |
| Black pepper | |

1. Preheat the air fryer to 160°C. Lightly coat the inside of four small oven-safe ramekins with rapeseed oil cooking spray. 2. Crack one egg into each ramekin, and season with salt and black pepper. 3. Place the ramekins into the air fryer basket. Close and set the timer to 7 minutes. 4. While the eggs are cooking, toast the bread in a toaster. 5. Slice the avocado in half lengthwise, remove the pit, and scoop the flesh into a small bowl. Season with salt, black pepper, and red pepper flakes, if desired. Using a fork, smash the avocado lightly. 6. Spread a quarter of the smashed avocado evenly over each slice of toast. 7. Remove the eggs from the air fryer, and gently spoon one onto each slice of avocado toast before serving.

# Breakfast Calzone

| | |
|---|---|
| 350 g grated Cheddar cheese | 230 g cooked sausage meat, removed from casings and crumbled |
| 60 g blanched finely ground almond flour | |
| 30 g full-fat soft cheese | 8 tablespoons grated mild Cheddar cheese |
| 1 large whole egg | |
| 4 large eggs, scrambled | |

1. In a large microwave-safe bowl, add Mozzarella, almond flour, and soft cheese. Microwave for 1 minute. Stir until the mixture is smooth and forms a ball. Add the egg and stir until dough forms. 2. Place dough between two sheets of parchment and roll out to ¼-inch thickness. Cut the dough into four rectangles. 3. Mix scrambled eggs and cooked sausage together in a large bowl. Divide the mixture evenly among each piece of dough, placing it on the lower half of the rectangle. Sprinkle each with 2 tablespoons Cheddar. 4. Fold over the rectangle to cover the egg and meat mixture. Pinch, roll, or use a wet fork to close the edges completely. 5. Cut a piece of parchment to fit your air fryer basket and place the calzones onto the parchment. Place parchment into the air fryer basket. 6. Adjust the temperature to 190°C and air fry for 15 minutes. 7. Flip the calzones halfway through the cooking time. When done, calzones should be golden in color. Serve immediately.

# Oat and Chia Porridge

| | |
|---|---|
| 2 tablespoons peanut butter | 1 L milk |
| 4 tablespoons honey | 475 g oats |
| 1 tablespoon butter, melted | 235 g chia seeds |

1. Preheat the air fryer to 200°C. 2. Put the peanut butter, honey, butter, and milk in a bowl and stir to mix. Add the oats and chia seeds and stir. 3. Transfer the mixture to a bowl and bake in the air fryer for 5 minutes. Give another stir before serving.

# Cinnamon Rolls

| | |
|---|---|
| 600 g grated Cheddar cheese | ½ teaspoon vanilla extract |
| 60 g soft cheese, softened | 96 ml icing sugar-style |
| 120 g blanched finely ground | sweetener |
| almond flour | 1 tablespoon ground cinnamon |

1. In a large microwave-safe bowl, combine Cheddar cheese, soft cheese, and flour. Microwave the mixture on high 90 seconds until cheese is melted. 2. Add vanilla extract and sweetener, and mix 2 minutes until a dough forms. 3. Once the dough is cool enough to work with your hands, about 2 minutes, spread it out into a 12 × 4-inch rectangle on ungreased parchment paper. Evenly sprinkle dough with cinnamon. 4. Starting at the long side of the dough, roll lengthwise to form a log. Slice the log into twelve even pieces. 5. Divide rolls between two ungreased round nonstick baking dishes. Place one dish into air fryer basket. Adjust the temperature to 190°C and bake for 10 minutes. 6. Cinnamon rolls will be done when golden around the edges and mostly firm. Repeat with second dish. Allow rolls to cool in dishes 10 minutes before serving.

# Spinach and Swiss Frittata with Mushrooms

| | |
|---|---|
| rapeseed oil cooking spray | 110 g baby mushrooms, sliced |
| 8 large eggs | 1 shallot, diced |
| ½ teaspoon salt | 120 g grated Swiss cheese, |
| ½ teaspoon black pepper | divided |
| 1 garlic clove, minced | Hot sauce, for serving (optional) |
| 475 g fresh baby spinach | |

1. Preheat the air fryer to 180°C. Lightly coat the inside of a 6-inch round cake pan with rapeseed oil cooking spray. 2. In a large bowl, beat the eggs, salt, pepper, and garlic for 1 to 2 minutes, or until well combined. 3. Fold in the spinach, mushrooms, shallot, and 60 ml the Swiss cheese. 4. Pour the egg mixture into the prepared cake pan, and sprinkle the remaining 60 ml Swiss over the top. 5. Place into the air fryer and bake for 18 to 20 minutes, or until the eggs are set in the center. 6. Remove from the air fryer and allow to cool for 5 minutes. Drizzle with hot sauce (if using) before serving.

# Cajun Breakfast Sausage

| | |
|---|---|
| 680 g 85% lean turkey mince | 1 teaspoon Cajun seasoning |
| 3 cloves garlic, finely chopped | 1 teaspoon dried thyme |
| ¼ onion, grated | ½ teaspoon paprika |
| 1 teaspoon Tabasco sauce | ½ teaspoon cayenne |

1. Preheat the air fryer to 190°C. 2. In a large bowl, combine the turkey, garlic, onion, Tabasco, Cajun seasoning, thyme, paprika, and cayenne. Mix with clean hands until thoroughly combined. Shape into 16 patties, about ½ inch thick. (Wet your hands slightly if you find the sausage too sticky to handle.) 3. Working in batches if necessary, arrange the patties in a single layer in the air fryer basket. Pausing halfway through the cooking time to flip the patties, air fry for 15 to 20 minutes until a thermometer inserted into the thickest portion registers 74°C.

# French Toast Sticks

| | |
|---|---|
| Oil, for spraying | 1 teaspoon ground cinnamon |
| 6 large eggs | 8 slices bread, cut into thirds |
| 315 ml milk | Syrup of choice, for serving |
| 2 teaspoons vanilla extract | |

1. Preheat the air fryer to 190°C. Line the air fryer basket with parchment and spray lightly with oil. 2. In a shallow bowl, whisk the eggs, milk, vanilla, and cinnamon. 3. Dunk one piece of bread in the egg mixture, making sure to coat both sides. Work quickly so the bread doesn't get soggy. Immediately transfer the bread to the prepared basket. 4. Repeat with the remaining bread, making sure the pieces don't touch each other. You may need to work in batches, depending on the size of your air fryer. 5. Air fry for 5 minutes, flip, and cook for another 3 to 4 minutes, until browned and crispy. 6. Serve immediately with your favourite syrup.

# Simple Scotch Eggs

**Prep time: 5 minutes | Cook time: 25 minutes | Serves 4**

4 large hard boiled eggs

1 (340 g) package pork sausage meat

8 slices streaky bacon

4 wooden cocktail sticks, soaked in water for at least 30 minutes

1. Slice the sausage meat into four parts and place each part into a large circle. 2. Put an egg into each circle and wrap it in the sausage. Put in the refrigerator for 1 hour. 3. Preheat the air fryer to 230°C. 4. Make a cross with two pieces of streaky bacon. Put a wrapped egg in the center, fold the bacon over top of the egg, and secure with a toothpick. 5. Air fry in the preheated air fryer for 25 minutes. 6. Serve immediately.

# Green Eggs and Ham

**Prep time: 5 minutes | Cook time: 10 minutes | Serves 2**

1 large Hass avocado, halved and pitted

2 thin slices ham

2 large eggs

2 tablespoons chopped spring onions, plus more for garnish

½ teaspoon fine sea salt

¼ teaspoon ground black pepper

60 g grated Cheddar cheese (omit for dairy-free)

1. Preheat the air fryer to 200°C. 2. Place a slice of ham into the cavity of each avocado half. Crack an egg on top of the ham, then sprinkle on the green onions, salt, and pepper. 3. Place the avocado halves in the air fryer cut side up and air fry for 10 minutes, or until the egg is cooked to your desired doneness. Top with the cheese (if using) and air fry for 30 seconds more, or until the cheese is melted. Garnish with chopped green onions. 4. Best served fresh. Store extras in an airtight container in the fridge for up to 4 days. Reheat in a preheated 180°C air fryer for a few minutes, until warmed through.

# Broccoli–Mushroom Frittata

**Prep time: 10 minutes | Cook time: 20 minutes | Serves 2**

1 tablespoon rapeseed oil

350 g broccoli florets, finely chopped

120 g sliced brown mushrooms

60 g finely chopped onion

½ teaspoon salt

¼ teaspoon freshly ground black pepper

6 eggs

60 g Parmesan cheese

1. In a nonstick cake pan, combine the rapeseed oil, broccoli, mushrooms, onion, salt, and pepper. Stir until the vegetables are thoroughly coated with oil. Place the cake pan in the air fryer basket and set the air fryer to 200°C. Air fry for 5 minutes until the vegetables soften. 2. Meanwhile, in a medium bowl, whisk the eggs and Parmesan until thoroughly combined. Pour the egg mixture into the pan and shake gently to distribute the vegetables. Air fry for another 15 minutes until the eggs are set. 3. Remove from the air fryer and let sit for 5 minutes to cool slightly. Use a silicone spatula to gently lift the frittata onto a plate before serving.

# Chapter 2 Family Favorites

# Chapter 2 Family Favorites

## Bacon–Wrapped Hot Dogs

### Prep time: 5 minutes | Cook time: 10 minutes | Serves 4

Oil, for spraying

4 bacon rashers

4 hot dog sausages

4 hot dog rolls

Toppings of choice

1. Line the air fryer basket with parchment and spray lightly with oil. 2.Wrap a strip of bacon tightly around each hot dog, taking care to cover the tips so they don't get too crispy. 3.Secure with a toothpick at each end to keep the bacon from shrinking. 4.Place the hot dogs in the prepared basket. 5.Air fry at 190°C for 8 to 9 minutes, depending on how crispy you like the bacon. For extra-crispy, cook the hot dogs at 200°C for 6 to 8 minutes. 6.Place the hot dogs in the buns, return them to the air fryer, and cook for another 1 to 2 minutes, or until the buns are warm. 7.Add your desired toppings and serve.

## Berry Cheesecake

### Prep time: 5 minutes | Cook time: 10 minutes | Serves 4

Oil, for spraying

227 g soft white cheese

6 tablespoons sugar

1 tablespoon sour cream

1 large egg

½ teaspoon vanilla extract

¼ teaspoon lemon juice

120 g fresh mixed berries

1. Preheat the air fryer to 180°C. 2.Line the air fryer basket with parchment and spray lightly with oil. 3.In a blender, combine the soft white cheese, sugar, sour cream, egg, vanilla, and lemon juice and blend until smooth. 4.Pour the mixture into a 4-inch springform pan. 5.Place the pan in the prepared basket. Cook for 8 to 10 minutes, or until only the very centre jiggles slightly when the pan is moved. 6.Refrigerate the cheesecake in the pan for at least 2 hours. 7.Release the sides from the springform pan, top the cheesecake with the mixed berries, and serve.

## Coconut Chicken Tenders

### Prep time: 10 minutes | Cook time: 12 minutes | Serves 4

Oil, for spraying

2 large eggs

60 ml milk

1 tablespoon chili sauce

350 g sweetened shredded

coconut

90 g Japanese breadcrumbs

1 teaspoon salt

½ teaspoon ground black

pepper

1. 450 g chicken tenders 2.Line the air fryer basket with parchment and spray lightly with oil. 3.In a small bowl, whisk together the eggs, milk, and chili sauce. 4.In a shallow dish, mix together the coconut, breadcrumbs, salt, and black pepper. 5.Coat the chicken in the egg mix, then dredge in the coconut mixture until evenly coated. 6.Place the chicken in the prepared basket and spray liberally with oil. 7.Air fry at 200°C for 6 minutes, flip, spray with more oil, and cook for another 6 minutes, or until the internal temperature reaches 74°C.

## Steak and Vegetable Kebabs

### Prep time: 15 minutes | Cook time: 5 to 7 minutes | Serves 4

2 tablespoons balsamic vinegar

2 teaspoons olive oil

½ teaspoon dried marjoram

⅛ teaspoon ground black

pepper

340 g silverside, cut into 1-inch pieces

1 red pepper, sliced

16 button mushrooms

235 g cherry tomatoes

1. In a medium bowl, stir together the balsamic vinegar, olive oil, marjoram, and black pepper. 2.Add the steak and stir to coat. Let stand for 10 minutes at room temperature. 3.Alternating items, thread the beef, red pepper, mushrooms, and tomatoes onto 8 bamboo or metal skewers that fit in the air fryer. 4.Air fry at 200°C for 5 to 7 minutes, or until the beef is browned and reaches at least 64°C on a meat thermometer. 5.Serve immediately.

## Beignets

**Prep time: 30 minutes | Cook time: 6 minutes | Makes 9 beignets**

Oil, for greasing and spraying
350 g plain flour, plus more for dusting
1½ teaspoons salt
1 (2¼-teaspoon) instant yeast
235 ml milk

2 tablespoons packed light muscovado sugar
1 tablespoon unsalted butter
1 large egg
180 g icing sugar

1. Oil a large bowl. In a small bowl, mix together the flour, salt, and yeast. Set aside. Pour the milk into a glass measuring cup and microwave in 1-minute intervals until it boils. 2.In a large bowl, mix together the brown sugar and butter. 3.Pour in the hot milk and whisk until the sugar has dissolved. Let cool to room temperature. 4.Whisk the egg into the cooled milk mixture and fold in the flour mixture until a dough form. 5.On a lightly floured work surface, knead the dough for 3 to 5 minutes. 6.Place the dough in the oiled bowl and cover with a clean kitchen towel. Let rise in a warm place for about 1 hour, or until doubled in size. 7.Roll the dough out on a lightly floured work surface until it's about ¼ inch thick. 8.Cut the dough into 3-inch squares and place them on a lightly floured baking sheet. 9.Cover loosely with a kitchen towel and let rise again until doubled in size, about 30 minutes. 10.Line the air fryer basket with parchment and spray lightly with oil. 11.Place the dough squares in the prepared basket and spray lightly with oil. You may need to work in batches, depending on the size of your air fryer. 12.Air fry at 200ºC for 3 minutes, flip, spray with oil, and cook for another 3 minutes, until crispy. 13.Dust with the icing sugar before serving.

## Mixed Berry Crumble

**Prep time: 10 minutes | Cook time: 11 to 16 minutes | Serves 4**

120 g chopped fresh strawberries
120 g fresh blueberries
80 g frozen raspberries
1 tablespoon freshly squeezed lemon juice

1 tablespoon honey
80 g wholemeal plain flour
3 tablespoons light muscovado sugar
2 tablespoons unsalted butter, melted

1. In a baking pan, combine the strawberries, blueberries, and raspberries. 2.Drizzle with the lemon juice and honey. 3.In a small bowl, mix the pastry flour and brown sugar. 4.Stir in the butter and mix until crumbly. 5.Sprinkle this mixture over the fruit. 6.Bake at 190ºC for 11 to 16 minutes, or until the fruit is tender and bubbly and the topping is golden brown. 7.Serve warm.

## Filo Vegetable Triangles

**Prep time: 15 minutes | Cook time: 6 to 11 minutes | Serves 6**

3 tablespoons finely chopped onion
2 garlic cloves, minced
2 tablespoons grated carrot
1 teaspoon olive oil
3 tablespoons frozen baby peas, thawed

2 tablespoons fat-free soft white cheese, at room temperature
6 sheets frozen filo pastry, thawed
Olive oil spray, for coating the dough

1. In a baking pan, combine the onion, garlic, carrot, and olive oil. 2.Air fry at 200ºC for 2 to 4 minutes, or until the vegetables are crisp-tender. 3.Transfer to a bowl. 4.Stir in the peas and soft white cheese to the vegetable mixture. Let cool while you prepare the dough. 5.Lay one sheet of filo on a work surface and lightly spray with olive oil spray. 6.Top with another sheet of filo. Repeat with the remaining 4 filo sheets; you'll have 3 stacks with 2 layers each. 7.Cut each stack lengthwise into 4 strips (12 strips total). Place a scant 2 teaspoons of the filling near the bottom of each strip. 8.Bring one corner up over the filling to make a triangle; continue folding the triangles over, as you would fold a flag. 9.Seal the edge with a bit of water. Repeat with the remaining strips and filling. 10.Air fry the triangles, in 2 batches, for 4 to 7 minutes, or until golden brown. Serve.

## Fish and Vegetable Tacos

**Prep time: 15 minutes | Cook time: 9 to 12 minutes | Serves 4**

450 g white fish fillets, such as sole or cod
2 teaspoons olive oil
3 tablespoons freshly squeezed lemon juice, divided
350 g chopped red cabbage

1 large carrot, grated
120 ml low-salt salsa
80 ml low-fat Greek yoghurt
4 soft low-salt wholemeal tortillas

1. Brush the fish with the olive oil and sprinkle with 1 tablespoon of lemon juice. 2.Air fry in the air fryer basket at 200ºC for 9 to 12 minutes, or until the fish just flakes when tested with a fork. 3.Meanwhile, in a medium bowl, stir together the remaining 2 tablespoons of lemon juice, the red cabbage, carrot, salsa, and yoghurt. 4.When the fish is cooked, remove it from the air fryer basket and break it up into large pieces. 5.Offer the fish, tortillas, and the cabbage mixture, and let each person assemble a taco.

# Meringue Cookies

**Prep time: 15 minutes | Cook time: 1 hour 30 minutes | Makes 20 cookies**

Oil, for spraying
4 large egg whites

185 g sugar
Pinch cream of tartar

1. Preheat the air fryer to 60°C. 2.Line the air fryer basket with parchment and spray lightly with oil. 3.In a small heatproof bowl, whisk together the egg whites and sugar. 4.Fill a small saucepan halfway with water, place it over medium heat, and bring to a light simmer. 5.Place the bowl with the egg whites on the saucepan, making sure the bottom of the bowl does not touch the water. 6.Whisk the mixture until the sugar is dissolved. Transfer the mixture to a large bowl and add the cream of tartar. 7.Using an electric mixer, beat the mixture on high until it is glossy and stiff peaks form. 8.Transfer the mixture to a piping bag or a zip-top plastic bag with a corner cut off. Pipe rounds into the prepared basket. 9.You may need to work in batches, depending on the size of your air fryer. Cook for 1 hour 30 minutes. 10.Turn off the air fryer and let the meringues cool completely inside. 11.The residual heat will continue to dry them out.

# Steak Tips and Potatoes

**Prep time: 10 minutes | Cook time: 20 minutes | Serves 4**

Oil, for spraying
227 g baby potatoes, cut in half
½ teaspoon salt
450 g steak, cut into ½-inch pieces

1 teaspoon Worcester sauce
1 teaspoon garlic powder
½ teaspoon salt
½ teaspoon ground black pepper

1. Line the air fryer basket with parchment and spray lightly with oil. 2.In a microwave-safe bowl, combine the potatoes and salt, then pour in about ½ inch of water. 3.Microwave for 7 minutes, or until the potatoes are nearly tender. Drain. 4.In a large bowl, gently mix together the steak, potatoes, Worcester sauce, garlic, salt, and black pepper. 5.Spread the mixture in an even layer in the prepared basket. Air fry at 200°C for 12 to 17 minutes, stirring after 5 to 6 minutes. 6.The cooking time will depend on the thickness of the meat and preferred doneness.

# Chapter 3 Fast and Easy Everyday Favourites

# Chapter 3 Fast and Easy Everyday Favourites

## Sweet Corn and Carrot Fritters

**Prep time: 10 minutes | Cook time: 8 to 11 minutes | Serves 4**

1 medium-sized carrot, grated
1 yellow onion, finely chopped
4 ounces (113 g) canned sweet corn kernels, drained
1 teaspoon sea salt flakes
1 tablespoon chopped fresh cilantro
1 medium-sized egg, whisked
2 tablespoons plain milk
1 cup grated Parmesan cheese
¼ cup flour
⅓ teaspoon baking powder
⅓ teaspoon sugar
Cooking spray

1. Preheat the air fryer to 350ºF (177ºC). 2. Place the grated carrot in a colander and press down to squeeze out any excess moisture. Dry it with a paper towel. 3. Combine the carrots with the remaining ingredients. 4. Mold 1 tablespoon of the mixture into a ball and press it down with your hand or a spoon to flatten it. Repeat until the rest of the mixture is used up. 5. Spritz the balls with cooking spray. 6. Arrange in the air fryer basket, taking care not to overlap any balls. Bake for 8 to 11 minutes, or until they're firm. 7. Serve warm.

## Simple Pea Delight

**Prep time: 5 minutes | Cook time: 15 minutes | Serves 2 to 4**

120 g flour
1 teaspoon baking powder
3 eggs
235 ml coconut milk
235 g soft white cheese
3 tablespoons pea protein
120 g chicken or turkey strips
Pinch of sea salt
235 g Mozzarella cheese

1. Preheat the air fryer to 200ºC. 2.In a large bowl, mix all ingredients together using a large wooden spoon. 3.Spoon equal amounts of the mixture into muffin cups and bake for 15 minutes. 4.Serve immediately.

## Crunchy Fried Okra

**Prep time: 5 minutes | Cook time: 8 to 10 minutes | Serves 4**

120 g self-raising yellow cornmeal (alternatively add 1 tablespoon baking powder to cornmeal)
1 teaspoon Italian-style seasoning
1 teaspoon paprika
1 teaspoon salt
½ teaspoon freshly ground black pepper
2 large eggs, beaten
475 g okra slices
Cooking spray

1. Preheat the air fryer to 200ºC. 2.Line the air fryer basket with parchment paper. In a shallow bowl, whisk the cornmeal, Italian-style seasoning, paprika, salt, and pepper until blended. 3.Place the beaten eggs in a second shallow bowl. Add the okra to the beaten egg and stir to coat. 4.Add the egg and okra mixture to the cornmeal mixture and stir until coated. 5.Place the okra on the parchment and spritz it with oil. 6.Air fry for 4 minutes. Shake the basket, spritz the okra with oil, and air fry for 4 to 6 minutes more until lightly browned and crispy. 7.Serve immediately.

## Air Fried Shishito Peppers

**Prep time: 5 minutes | Cook time: 5 minutes | Serves 4**

230 g shishito or Padron peppers (about 24)
1 tablespoon olive oil
Coarse sea salt, to taste
Lemon wedges, for serving
Cooking spray

1. Preheat the air fryer to 200ºC. 2.Spritz the air fryer basket with cooking spray. 3.Toss the peppers with olive oil in a large bowl to coat well. Arrange the peppers in the preheated air fryer. 4.Air fryer for 5 minutes or until blistered and lightly charred. Shake the basket and sprinkle the peppers with salt halfway through the cooking time. 5.Transfer the peppers onto a plate and squeeze the lemon wedges on top before serving.

# Rosemary and Orange Roasted Chickpeas

**Prep time: 5 minutes | Cook time: 10 to 12 minutes | Makes 1 L**

| | |
|---|---|
| 1 kg cooked chickpeas | 1 teaspoon paprika |
| 2 tablespoons vegetable oil | Zest of 1 orange |
| 1 teaspoon rock salt | 1 tablespoon chopped fresh |
| 1 teaspoon cumin | rosemary |

1. Preheat the air fryer to 200ºC. 2.Make sure the chickpeas are completely dry prior to roasting. In a medium bowl, toss the chickpeas with oil, salt, cumin, and paprika. 3.Working in batches, spread the chickpeas in a single layer in the air fryer basket. 4.Air fry for 10 to 12 minutes until crisp, shaking once halfway through. 5.Return the warm chickpeas to the bowl and toss with the orange zest and rosemary. 6.Allow to cool completely. Serve.

# Herb–Roasted Veggies

**Prep time: 10 minutes | Cook time: 14 to 18 minutes | Serves 4**

| | |
|---|---|
| 1 red pepper, sliced | 80 g diced red onion |
| 1 (230 g) package sliced | 3 garlic cloves, sliced |
| mushrooms | 1 teaspoon olive oil |
| 235 g green beans, cut into | ½ teaspoon dried basil |
| 2-inch pieces | ½ teaspoon dried tarragon |

1. Preheat the air fryer to 180ºC. 2.In a medium bowl, mix the red pepper, mushrooms, green beans, red onion, and garlic. 3.Drizzle with the olive oil. Toss to coat. 4.Add the herbs and toss again. Place the vegetables in the air fryer basket. 5.Roast for 14 to 18 minutes, or until tender. 6.Serve immediately.

# Simple and Easy Croutons

**Prep time: 5 minutes | Cook time: 8 minutes | Serves 4**

| | |
|---|---|
| 2 sliced bread | Hot soup, for serving |
| 1 tablespoon olive oil | |

1. Preheat the air fryer to 200ºC. 2.Cut the slices of bread into medium-size chunks. 3.Brush the air fryer basket with the oil. 4.Place the chunks inside and air fry for at least 8 minutes. 5.Serve with hot soup.

# Baked Halloumi with Greek Salsa

**Prep time: 15 minutes | Cook time: 6 minutes | Serves 4**

Salsa:
| | |
|---|---|
| 1 small shallot, finely diced | finely diced |
| 3 garlic cloves, minced | 2 teaspoons chopped fresh |
| 2 tablespoons fresh lemon juice | parsley |
| 2 tablespoons extra-virgin olive | 1 teaspoon snipped fresh dill |
| oil | 1 teaspoon snipped fresh |
| 1 teaspoon freshly cracked | oregano |
| black pepper | Cheese: |
| Pinch of rock salt | 227 g Halloumi cheese, sliced |
| 120 ml finely diced English | into ½-inch-thick pieces |
| cucumber | 1 tablespoon extra-virgin olive |
| 1 plum tomato, deseeded and | oil |

Preheat the air fryer to 192ºC. For the salsa: Combine the shallot, garlic, lemon juice, olive oil, pepper, and salt in a medium bowl. Add the cucumber, tomato, parsley, dill, and oregano. Toss gently to combine; set aside. For the cheese: Place the cheese slices in a medium bowl. Drizzle with the olive oil. Toss gently to coat. Arrange the cheese in a single layer in the air fryer basket. Bake for 6 minutes. Divide the cheese among four serving plates. Top with the salsa and serve immediately.

# Air Fried Courgette Sticks

**Prep time: 5 minutes | Cook time: 20 minutes | Serves 4**

| | |
|---|---|
| 1 medium courgette, cut into 48 | 1 tablespoon melted margarine |
| sticks | Cooking spray |
| 30 g seasoned breadcrumbs | |

1. Preheat the air fryer to 180ºC. Spritz the air fryer basket with cooking spray and set aside. In 2 different shallow bowls, add the seasoned breadcrumbs and the margarine. One by one, dredge the courgette sticks into the margarine, then roll in the breadcrumbs to coat evenly. Arrange the crusted sticks on a plate. Place the courgette sticks in the prepared air fryer basket. Work in two batches to avoid overcrowding. Air fry for 10 minutes, or until golden brown and crispy. Shake the basket halfway through to cook evenly. When the cooking time is over, transfer the fries to a wire rack. Rest for 5 minutes and serve warm.

# Cheesy Chilli Toast

**Prep time: 5 minutes | Cook time: 5 minutes | Serves 1**

2 tablespoons grated Parmesan
cheese
2 tablespoons grated Mozzarella
cheese
2 teaspoons salted butter, at

room temperature
10 to 15 thin slices serrano
chilli or jalapeño
2 slices sourdough bread
½ teaspoon black pepper

1. Preheat the air fryer to 160°C. 2.In a small bowl, stir together the Parmesan, Mozzarella, butter, and chillies. 3.Spread half the mixture onto one side of each slice of bread. 4.Sprinkle with the pepper. 5.Place the slices, cheese-side up, in the air fryer basket. 6.Bake for 5 minutes, or until the cheese has melted and started to brown slightly. 7.Serve immediately.

# Buttery Sweet Potatoes

**Prep time: 5 minutes | Cook time: 10 minutes | Serves 4**

2 tablespoons melted butter
1 tablespoon light brown sugar
2 sweet potatoes, peeled and cut

into ½-inch cubes
Cooking spray

1. Preheat the air fryer to 200°C. 2.Line the air fryer basket with parchment paper. In a medium bowl, stir together the melted butter and brown sugar until blended. 3.Toss the sweet potatoes in the butter mixture until coated. Place the sweet potatoes on the parchment and spritz with oil. 4.Air fry for 5 minutes. Shake the basket, spritz the sweet potatoes with oil, and air fry for 5 minutes more until they're soft enough to cut with a fork. 5.Serve immediately.

# Traditional Queso Fundido

**Prep time: 10 minutes | Cook time: 25 minutes | Serves 4**

110 g fresh Mexican (or
Spanish if unavailable) chorizo,
casings removed
1 medium onion, chopped
3 cloves garlic, minced
235 g chopped tomato
2 jalapeños, deseeded and diced
2 teaspoons ground cumin

475 g shredded Oaxaca or
Mozzarella cheese
120 ml half-and-half (60 g
whole milk and 60 ml cream
combined)
Celery sticks or tortilla chips,
for serving

1. Preheat the air fryer to 200°C. 2.In a baking tray, combine the chorizo, onion, garlic, tomato, jalapeños, and cumin. Stir to combine. 3.Place the pan in the air fryer basket. 4.Air fry for 15 minutes, or until the sausage is cooked, stirring halfway through the cooking time to break up the sausage. 5.Add the cheese and half-and-half; stir to combine. 6.Air fry for 10 minutes, or until the cheese has melted. 7.Serve with celery sticks or tortilla chips.

# Baked Chorizo Scotch Eggs

**Prep time:5 minutes | Cook time: 15 to 20 minutes | Makes 4 eggs**

450 g Mexican chorizo or other
seasoned sausage meat
4 soft-boiled eggs plus 1 raw
egg

1 tablespoon water
120 ml plain flour
235 ml panko breadcrumbs
Cooking spray

1. Divide the chorizo into 4 equal portions. Flatten each portion into a disc. Place a soft-boiled egg in the centre of each disc. Wrap the chorizo around the egg, encasing it completely. Place the encased eggs on a plate and chill for at least 30 minutes. 2.Preheat the air fryer to 182°C. 3.Beat the raw egg with 1 tablespoon of water. Place the flour on a small plate and the panko on a second plate. Working with 1 egg at a time, roll the encased egg in the flour, then dip it in the egg mixture. Dredge the egg in the panko and place on a plate. Repeat with the remaining eggs. 4.Spray the eggs with oil and place in the air fryer basket. Bake for 10 minutes. Turn and bake for an additional 5 to 10 minutes, or until browned and crisp on all sides. 5.Serve immediately.

# Easy Devils on Horseback

**Prep time: 5 minutes | Cook time: 7 minutes | Serves 12**

24 small pitted prunes (128 g)
60 g crumbled blue cheese,
divided

8 slices centre-cut bacon, cut
crosswise into thirds

1. Preheat the air fryer to 200°C. 2.Halve the prunes lengthwise, but don't cut them all the way through. 3.Place ½ teaspoon of cheese in the centre of each prune. 4.Wrap a piece of bacon around each prune and secure the bacon with a toothpick. 5.Working in batches, arrange a single layer of the prunes in the air fryer basket. 6.Air fry for about 7 minutes, flipping halfway, until the bacon is cooked through and crisp. 7.Let cool slightly and serve warm.

# Bacon Pinwheels

**Prep time: 10 minutes | Cook time: 10 minutes | Makes 8 pinwheels**

1 sheet puff pastry
2 tablespoons maple syrup
48 g brown sugar

8 slices bacon
Ground black pepper, to taste
Cooking spray

Preheat the air fryer to 180°C. Spritz the air fryer basket with cooking spray. Roll the puff pastry into a 10-inch square with a rolling pin on a clean work surface, then cut the pastry into 8 strips. Brush the strips with maple syrup and sprinkle with sugar, leaving a 1-inch far end uncovered. Arrange each slice of bacon on each strip, leaving a ⅛-inch length of bacon hang over the end close to you. Sprinkle with black pepper. From the end close to you, roll the strips into pinwheels, then dab the uncovered end with water and seal the rolls. Arrange the pinwheels in the preheated air fryer and spritz with cooking spray. Air fry for 10 minutes or until golden brown. Flip the pinwheels halfway through. Serve immediately.

# Chapter 4 Poultry

# Chapter 4 Poultry

## Cornish Hens with Honey–Lime Glaze

**Prep time: 15 minutes | Cook time: 25 to 30 minutes | Serves 2 to 3**

| | |
|---|---|
| 1 small chicken (680 to 900 g) | 1 teaspoon poultry seasoning |
| 1 tablespoon honey | Salt and pepper, to taste |
| 1 tablespoon lime juice | Cooking spray |

1. To split the chicken into halves, cut through breast bone and down one side of the backbone. 2. Mix the honey, lime juice, and poultry seasoning together and brush or rub onto all sides of the chicken. Season to taste with salt and pepper. 3. Spray the air fryer basket with cooking spray and place hen halves in the basket, skin-side down. 4. Air fry at 170ºC for 25 to 30 minutes. Chicken will be done when juices run clear when pierced at leg joint with a fork. Let chicken rest for 5 to 10 minutes before cutting.

## Korean Honey Wings

**Prep time: 10 minutes | Cook time: 25 minutes per batch | Serves 4**

| | |
|---|---|
| 55 g gochujang, or red pepper paste | 2 teaspoons ground ginger |
| 55 g mayonnaise | 1.4 kg whole chicken wings |
| 2 tablespoons honey | Olive oil spray |
| 1 tablespoon sesame oil | 1 teaspoon salt |
| 2 teaspoons minced garlic | ½ teaspoon freshly ground black pepper |
| 1 tablespoon sugar | |

1. In a large bowl, whisk the gochujang, mayonnaise, honey, sesame oil, garlic, sugar, and ginger. Set aside. 2. Insert the crisper plate into the basket and the basket into the unit. Preheat the unit by selecting AIR FRY, setting the temperature to 200ºC, and setting the time to 3 minutes. Select START/STOP to begin. 3. To prepare the chicken wings, cut the wings in half. The meatier part is the drumette. Cut off and discard the wing tip from the flat part (or save the wing tips in the freezer to make chicken stock). 4. Once the unit is preheated, spray the crisper plate with olive oil. Working in batches, place half the chicken wings into the basket, spray them with olive oil, and sprinkle with the salt and pepper.

5. Select AIR FRY, set the temperature to 200ºC, and set the time to 20 minutes. Select START/STOP to begin. 6. After 10 minutes, remove the basket, flip the wings, and spray them with more olive oil. Reinsert the basket to resume cooking. 7. Cook the wings to an internal temperature of 76ºC, then transfer them to the bowl with the prepared sauce and toss to coat. 8. Repeat steps 4, 5, 6, and 7 for the remaining chicken wings. 9. Return the coated wings to the basket and air fry for 4 to 6 minutes more until the sauce has glazed the wings and the chicken is crisp. After 3 minutes, check the wings to make sure they aren't burning. Serve hot.

## Bacon Lovers Ⓩ Stuffed Chicken

**Prep time: 15 minutes | Cook time: 10 minutes | Serves 4**

| | |
|---|---|
| 4 (140 g) boneless, skinless chicken breasts, pounded to ¼ inch thick | softened, for dairy-free) |
| | 8 slices thin-cut bacon or beef bacon |
| 2 (150 g) packages Boursin cheese (or Kite Hill brand chive cream cheese style spread, | Sprig of fresh coriander, for garnish (optional) |

1. Spray the air fryer basket with avocado oil. Preheat the air fryer to 200ºC. 2. Place one of the chicken breasts on a cutting board. With a sharp knife held parallel to the cutting board, make a 1-inch-wide incision at the top of the breast. Carefully cut into the breast to form a large pocket, leaving a ½-inch border along the sides and bottom. Repeat with the other 3 chicken breasts. 3. Snip the corner of a large resealable plastic bag to form a ¾-inch hole. Place the Boursin cheese in the bag and pipe the cheese into the pockets in the chicken breasts, dividing the cheese evenly among them. 4. Wrap 2 slices of bacon around each chicken breast and secure the ends with toothpicks. Place the bacon-wrapped chicken in the air fryer basket and air fry until the bacon is crisp and the chicken's internal temperature reaches 76ºC, about 18 to 20 minutes, flipping after 10 minutes. Garnish with a sprig of coriander before serving, if desired. 5. Store leftovers in an airtight container in the refrigerator for up to 4 days. Reheat in a preheated 200ºC air fryer for 5 minutes, or until warmed through.

## Chicken Shawarma

Shawarma Spice:
2 teaspoons dried oregano
1 teaspoon ground cinnamon
1 teaspoon ground cumin
1 teaspoon ground coriander
1 teaspoon kosher salt
½ teaspoon ground allspice
½ teaspoon cayenne pepper

Chicken:
450 g boneless, skinless chicken thighs, cut into large bite-size chunks
2 tablespoons vegetable oil
For Serving:
Tzatziki
Pita bread

1. For the shawarma spice: In a small bowl, combine the oregano, cayenne, cumin, coriander, salt, cinnamon, and allspice. 2. For the chicken: In a large bowl, toss together the chicken, vegetable oil, and shawarma spice to coat. Marinate at room temperature for 30 minutes or cover and refrigerate for up to 24 hours. 3. Place the chicken in the air fryer basket. Set the air fryer to 180°C for 15 minutes, or until the chicken reaches an internal temperature of 76°C. 4. Transfer the chicken to a serving platter. Serve with tzatziki and pita bread.

## Fried Chicken Breasts

450 g boneless, skinless chicken breasts
180 ml dill pickle juice
35 g finely ground blanched almond flour
70 g finely grated Parmesan

cheese
½ teaspoon sea salt
½ teaspoon freshly ground black pepper
2 large eggs
Avocado oil spray

1. Place the chicken breasts in a zip-top bag or between two pieces of plastic wrap. Using a meat mallet or heavy skillet, pound the chicken to a uniform ½-inch thickness. 2. Place the chicken in a large bowl with the pickle juice. Cover and allow to brine in the refrigerator for up to 2 hours. 3. In a shallow dish, combine the almond flour, Parmesan cheese, salt, and pepper. In a separate, shallow bowl, beat the eggs. 4. Drain the chicken and pat it dry with paper towels. Dip in the eggs and then in the flour mixture, making sure to press the coating into the chicken. Spray both sides of the coated breasts with oil. 5. Spray the air fryer basket with oil and put the chicken inside. Set the temperature to 200°C and air fry for 6 to 7 minutes. 6. Carefully flip the breasts with a spatula. Spray the breasts again with oil and continue cooking for 6 to 7 minutes more, until golden and crispy.

## Pecan Turkey Cutlets

45 g panko bread crumbs
¼ teaspoon salt
¼ teaspoon pepper
¼ teaspoon mustard powder
¼ teaspoon poultry seasoning
50 g pecans

15 g cornflour
1 egg, beaten
450 g turkey cutlets, ½-inch thick
Salt and pepper, to taste
Oil for misting or cooking spray

1. Place the panko crumbs, ¼ teaspoon salt, ¼ teaspoon pepper, mustard, and poultry seasoning in food processor. Process until crumbs are finely crushed. Add pecans and process in short pulses just until nuts are finely chopped. Go easy so you don't overdo it! 2. Preheat the air fryer to 180°C. 3. Place cornflour in one shallow dish and beaten egg in another. Transfer coating mixture from food processor into a third shallow dish. 4. Sprinkle turkey cutlets with salt and pepper to taste. 5. Dip cutlets in cornflour and shake off excess. Then dip in beaten egg and roll in crumbs, pressing to coat well. Spray both sides with oil or cooking spray. 6. Place 2 cutlets in air fryer basket in a single layer and cook for 10 to 12 minutes or until juices run clear. 7. Repeat step 6 to cook remaining cutlets.

## Herbed Roast Chicken Breast

2 tablespoons salted butter or ghee, at room temperature
1 teaspoon dried Italian seasoning, crushed
½ teaspoon kosher salt

½ teaspoon smoked paprika
¼ teaspoon black pepper
2 bone-in, skin-on chicken breast halves (280 g each)
Lemon wedges, for serving

1. In a small bowl, stir together the butter, Italian seasoning, salt, paprika, and pepper until thoroughly combined. 2. Using a small sharp knife, carefully loosen the skin on each chicken breast half, starting at the thin end of each. Very carefully separate the skin from the flesh, leaving the skin attached at the thick end of each breast. Divide the herb butter into quarters. Rub one-quarter of the butter onto the flesh of each breast. Fold and lightly press the skin back onto each breast. Rub the remaining butter onto the skin of each breast. 3. Place the chicken in the air fryer basket. Set the air fryer to (190°C for 25 minutes. Use a meat thermometer to ensure the chicken breasts have reached an internal temperature of 76°C. 4. Transfer the chicken to a cutting board. Lightly cover with aluminum foil and let rest for 5 to 10 minutes. 5. Serve with lemon wedges.

# Chicken Pesto Parmigiana

**Prep time: 10 minutes | Cook time: 23 minutes | Serves 4**

| | |
|---|---|
| 2 large eggs | pounded to ¼ inch thick |
| 1 tablespoon water | 65 g pesto |
| Fine sea salt and ground black pepper, to taste | 115 g shredded Mozzarella cheese |
| 45 g powdered Parmesan cheese | Finely chopped fresh basil, for garnish (optional) |
| 2 teaspoons Italian seasoning | Grape tomatoes, halved, for serving (optional) |
| 4 (140 g) boneless, skinless chicken breasts or thighs, | |

1. Spray the air fryer basket with avocado oil. Preheat the air fryer to 200°C. 2. Crack the eggs into a shallow baking dish, add the water and a pinch each of salt and pepper, and whisk to combine. In another shallow baking dish, stir together the Parmesan and Italian seasoning until well combined. 3. Season the chicken breasts well on both sides with salt and pepper. Dip one chicken breast in the eggs and let any excess drip off, then dredge both sides of the breast in the Parmesan mixture. Spray the breast with avocado oil and place it in the air fryer basket. Repeat with the remaining 3 chicken breasts. 4. Air fry the chicken in the air fryer for 20 minutes, or until the internal temperature reaches 76°C and the breading is golden brown, flipping halfway through. 5. Dollop each chicken breast with ¼ of the pesto and top with the Mozzarella. Return the breasts to the air fryer and cook for 3 minutes, or until the cheese is melted. Garnish with basil and serve with halved grape tomatoes on the side, if desired. 6. Store leftovers in an airtight container in the refrigerator for up to 4 days. Reheat in a preheated 200°C air fryer for 5 minutes, or until warmed through.

# Chicken, Courgette, and Spinach Salad

**Prep time: 10 minutes | Cook time: 20 minutes | Serves 4**

| | |
|---|---|
| 3 (140 g) boneless, skinless chicken breasts, cut into 1-inch cubes | 1 medium red onion, sliced |
| | 1 red bell pepper, sliced |
| | 1 small courgette, cut into strips |
| 5 teaspoons extra-virgin olive oil | 3 tablespoons freshly squeezed lemon juice |
| ½ teaspoon dried thyme | 85 g fresh baby spinach leaves |

1. Insert the crisper plate into the basket and the basket into the unit. Preheat the unit by selecting AIR ROAST, setting the temperature to 190°C, and setting the time to 3 minutes. Select START/STOP to begin. 2. In a large bowl, combine the chicken, olive oil, and thyme. Toss to coat. Transfer to a medium metal bowl that fits into the basket. 3. Once the unit is preheated, place the bowl into the basket. 4. Select AIR ROAST, set the temperature to 190°C, and set the time to 20 minutes. Select START/STOP to begin. 5. After 8 minutes, add the red onion, red bell pepper, and courgette to the bowl. Resume cooking. After about 6 minutes more, stir the chicken and vegetables. Resume cooking. 6. When the cooking is complete, a food thermometer inserted into the chicken should register at least 76°C. Remove the bowl from the unit and stir in the lemon juice. 7. Put the spinach in a serving bowl and top with the chicken mixture. Toss to combine and serve immediately.

# Garlic Dill Wings

**Prep time: 5 minutes | Cook time: 25 minutes | Serves 4**

| | |
|---|---|
| 900 g bone-in chicken wings, separated at joints | pepper |
| | ½ teaspoon onion powder |
| ½ teaspoon salt | ½ teaspoon garlic powder |
| ½ teaspoon ground black | 1 teaspoon dried dill |

1. In a large bowl, toss wings with salt, pepper, onion powder, garlic powder, and dill until evenly coated. Place wings into ungreased air fryer basket in a single layer, working in batches if needed. 2. Adjust the temperature to 200°C and air fry for 25 minutes, shaking the basket every 7 minutes during cooking. Wings should have an internal temperature of at least 76°C and be golden brown when done. Serve warm.

# Ham Chicken with Cheese

**Prep time: 15 minutes | Cook time: 25 minutes | Serves 4**

| | |
|---|---|
| 55 g unsalted butter, softened | 60 ml water |
| 115 g cream cheese, softened | 280 g shredded cooked chicken |
| 1½ teaspoons Dijon mustard | 115 g ham, chopped |
| 2 tablespoons white wine vinegar | 115 g sliced Swiss or Provolone cheese |

1. Preheat the air fryer to 190°C. Lightly coat a casserole dish that will fit in the air fryer, such as an 8-inch round pan, with olive oil and set aside. 2. In a large bowl and using an electric mixer, combine the butter, cream cheese, Dijon mustard, and vinegar. With the motor running at low speed, slowly add the water and beat until smooth. Set aside. 3. Arrange an even layer of chicken in the bottom of the prepared pan, followed by the ham. Spread the butter and cream cheese mixture on top of the ham, followed by the cheese slices on the top layer. Air fry for 20 to 25 minutes until warmed through and the cheese has browned.

# Chicken Wings with Piri Piri Sauce

**Prep time: 30 minutes | Cook time: 30 minutes |**
### Serves 6

| | |
|---|---|
| 12 chicken wings | and chopped |
| 45 g butter, melted | 1 tablespoon pimiento, seeded |
| 1 teaspoon onion powder | and minced |
| ½ teaspoon cumin powder | 1 garlic clove, chopped |
| 1 teaspoon garlic paste | 2 tablespoons fresh lemon juice |
| Sauce: | ⅓ teaspoon sea salt |
| 60 g piri piri peppers, stemmed | ½ teaspoon tarragon |

1. Steam the chicken wings using a steamer basket that is placed over a saucepan with boiling water; reduce the heat. 2. Now, steam the wings for 10 minutes over a moderate heat. Toss the wings with butter, onion powder, cumin powder, and garlic paste. 3. Let the chicken wings cool to room temperature. Then, refrigerate them for 45 to 50 minutes. 4. Roast in the preheated air fryer at 170°C for 25 to 30 minutes; make sure to flip them halfway through. 5. While the chicken wings are cooking, prepare the sauce by mixing all of the sauce ingredients in a food processor. Toss the wings with prepared Piri Piri Sauce and serve.

# Coconut Chicken Wings with Mango Sauce

**Prep time: 15 minutes | Cook time: 20 minutes |**
### Serves 4

| | |
|---|---|
| 16 chicken drumettes (party wings) | coconut |
| 60 ml full-fat coconut milk | 30 g all-purpose flour |
| 1 tablespoon sriracha | Cooking oil spray |
| 1 teaspoon onion powder | 165 g mango, cut into ½-inch |
| 1 teaspoon garlic powder | chunks |
| Salt and freshly ground black | 15 g fresh coriander, chopped |
| pepper, to taste | 25 g red onion, chopped |
| 25 g shredded unsweetened | 2 garlic cloves, minced |
| | Juice of ½ lime |

1. Place the drumettes in a resealable plastic bag. 2. In a small bowl, whisk the coconut milk and sriracha. 3. Drizzle the drumettes with the sriracha–coconut milk mixture. Season the drumettes with the onion powder, garlic powder, salt, and pepper. Seal the bag. Shake it thoroughly to combine the seasonings and coat the chicken. Marinate for at least 30 minutes, preferably overnight, in the refrigerator. 4. When the drumettes are almost done marinating, in a large bowl, stir together the shredded coconut and flour. 5. Dip the drumettes into the coconut-flour mixture. Press the flour mixture onto the chicken with your hands. 6. Insert the crisper plate into the basket and the basket into the unit. Preheat the unit by selecting AIR FRY, setting the temperature to 200°C, and setting the time to 3 minutes. Select START/STOP to begin. 7. Once the unit is preheated, spray the crisper plate and the basket with cooking oil. Place the drumettes in the air fryer. It is okay to stack them. Spray the drumettes with cooking oil, being sure to cover the bottom layer. 8. Select AIR FRY, set the temperature to 200°C, and set the time to 20 minutes. Select START/STOP to begin. 9. After 5 minutes, remove the basket and shake it to ensure all pieces cook through. Reinsert the basket to resume cooking. Remove and shake the basket every 5 minutes, twice more, until a food thermometer inserted into the drumettes registers 76°C. 10. When the cooking is complete, let the chicken cool for 5 minutes. 11. While the chicken cooks and cools, make the salsa. In a small bowl, combine the mango, coriander, red onion, garlic, and lime juice. Mix well until fully combined. Serve with the wings.

# Israeli Chicken Schnitzel

**Prep time: 5 minutes | Cook time: 10 minutes |**
### Serves 4

| | |
|---|---|
| 2 large boneless, skinless | 1 teaspoon paprika |
| chicken breasts, each weighing | 2 eggs beaten with 2 |
| about 450 g | tablespoons water |
| 65 g all-purpose flour | 125 g panko bread crumbs |
| 2 teaspoons garlic powder | Vegetable oil spray |
| 2 teaspoons kosher salt | Lemon juice, for serving |
| 1 teaspoon black pepper | |

1. Preheat the air fryer to 190°C. 2. Place 1 chicken breast between 2 pieces of plastic wrap. Use a mallet or a rolling pin to pound the chicken until it is ¼ inch thick. Set aside. Repeat with the second breast. Whisk together the flour, garlic powder, salt, pepper, and paprika on a large plate. Place the panko in a separate shallow bowl or pie plate. 3. Dredge 1 chicken breast in the flour, shaking off any excess, then dip it in the egg mixture. Dredge the chicken breast in the panko, making sure to coat it completely. Shake off any excess panko. Place the battered chicken breast on a plate. Repeat with the second chicken breast. 4. Spray the air fryer basket with oil spray. Place 1 of the battered chicken breasts in the basket and spray the top with oil spray. Air fry until the top is browned, about 5 minutes. Flip the chicken and spray the second side with oil spray. Air fry until the second side is browned and crispy and the internal temperature reaches 76°C. Remove the first chicken breast from the air fryer and repeat with the second chicken breast. 5. Serve hot with lemon juice.

# Yellow Curry Chicken Thighs with Peanuts

**Prep time: 10 minutes | Cook time: 20 minutes | Serves 6**

| | |
|---|---|
| 120 ml unsweetened full-fat coconut milk | 1 tablespoon minced garlic |
| 2 tablespoons yellow curry paste | 1 teaspoon kosher salt |
| 1 tablespoon minced fresh ginger | 450 g boneless, skinless chicken thighs, halved crosswise |
| | 2 tablespoons chopped peanuts |

1. In a large bowl, stir together the coconut milk, curry paste, ginger, garlic, and salt until well blended. Add the chicken; toss well to coat. Marinate at room temperature for 30 minutes, or cover and refrigerate for up to 24 hours. 2. Preheat the air fryer to 190ºC. 3. Place the chicken (along with marinade) in a baking pan. Place the pan in the air fryer basket. Bake for 20 minutes, turning the chicken halfway through the cooking time. Use a meat thermometer to ensure the chicken has reached an internal temperature of 76ºC. 4. Sprinkle the chicken with the chopped peanuts and serve.

# Chicken Rochambeau

**Prep time: 15 minutes | Cook time: 20 minutes | Serves 4**

| | |
|---|---|
| 1 tablespoon butter | Sauce: |
| 4 chicken tenders, cut in half crosswise | 2 tablespoons butter |
| Salt and pepper, to taste | 25 g chopped green onions |
| 15 g flour | 50 g chopped mushrooms |
| Oil for misting | 2 tablespoons flour |
| 4 slices ham, ¼- to ⅜-inches thick and large enough to cover an English muffin | 240 ml chicken broth |
| | ¼ teaspoon garlic powder |
| 2 English muffins, split | 1½ teaspoons Worcestershire sauce |

1. Place 1 tablespoon of butter in a baking pan and air fry at 200ºC for 2 minutes to melt. 2. Sprinkle chicken tenders with salt and pepper to taste, then roll in the flour. 3. Place chicken in baking pan, turning pieces to coat with melted butter. 4. Air fry at 200ºC for 5 minutes. Turn chicken pieces over, and spray tops lightly with olive oil. Cook 5 minutes longer or until juices run clear. The chicken will not brown. 5. While chicken is cooking, make the sauce: In a medium saucepan, melt the 2 tablespoons of butter. 6. Add onions and mushrooms and sauté until tender, about 3 minutes. 7. Stir in the flour. Gradually add broth, stirring constantly until you have a smooth gravy. 8. Add garlic powder and Worcestershire sauce and simmer on low heat until sauce thickens, about 5 minutes. 9.

When chicken is cooked, remove baking pan from air fryer and set aside. 10. Place ham slices directly into air fryer basket and air fry at 200ºC for 5 minutes or until hot and beginning to sizzle a little. Remove and set aside on top of the chicken for now. 11. Place the English muffin halves in air fryer basket and air fry at 200ºC for 1 minute. 12. Open air fryer and place a ham slice on top of each English muffin half. Stack 2 pieces of chicken on top of each ham slice. Air fry for 1 to 2 minutes to heat through. 13. Place each English muffin stack on a serving plate and top with plenty of sauce.

# Ginger Turmeric Chicken Thighs

**Prep time: 5 minutes | Cook time: 25 minutes | Serves 4**

| | |
|---|---|
| 4 (115 g) boneless, skin-on chicken thighs | ½ teaspoon salt |
| 2 tablespoons coconut oil, melted | ½ teaspoon garlic powder |
| | ½ teaspoon ground ginger |
| ½ teaspoon ground turmeric | ¼ teaspoon ground black pepper |

1. Place chicken thighs in a large bowl and drizzle with coconut oil. Sprinkle with remaining ingredients and toss to coat both sides of thighs. 2. Place thighs skin side up into ungreased air fryer basket. Adjust the temperature to 200ºC and air fry for 25 minutes. After 10 minutes, turn thighs. When 5 minutes remain, flip thighs once more. Chicken will be done when skin is golden brown and the internal temperature is at least 76ºC. Serve warm.

# Blackened Chicken

**Prep time: 10 minutes | Cook time: 20 minutes | Serves 4**

| | |
|---|---|
| 1 large egg, beaten | chicken breasts (about 450 g each), halved |
| 215 g Blackened seasoning | |
| 2 whole boneless, skinless | 1 to 2 tablespoons oil |

1. Place the beaten egg in one shallow bowl and the Blackened seasoning in another shallow bowl. 2. One at a time, dip the chicken pieces in the beaten egg and the Blackened seasoning, coating thoroughly. 3. Preheat the air fryer to 180ºC. Line the air fryer basket with parchment paper. 4. Place the chicken pieces on the parchment and spritz with oil. 5. Cook for 10 minutes. Flip the chicken, spritz it with oil, and cook for 10 minutes more until the internal temperature reaches 76ºC and the chicken is no longer pink inside. Let sit for 5 minutes before serving.

# Cheesy Pepperoni and Chicken Pizza

**Prep time: 15 minutes | Cook time: 15 minutes |**

**Serves 6**

280 g cooked chicken, cubed
240 g pizza sauce
20 slices pepperoni
20 g grated Parmesan cheese

225 g shredded Mozzarella cheese
Cooking spray

1. Preheat the air fryer to 190ºC. Spritz a baking pan with cooking spray. 2. Arrange the chicken cubes in the prepared baking pan, then top the cubes with pizza sauce and pepperoni. Stir to coat the cubes and pepperoni with sauce. 3. Scatter the cheeses on top, then place the baking pan in the preheated air fryer. Air fryer for 15 minutes or until frothy and the cheeses melt. 4. Serve immediately.

# Greek Chicken Stir–Fry

**Prep time: 15 minutes | Cook time: 15 minutes |**

**Serves 2**

1 (170 g) chicken breast, cut into 1-inch cubes
½ medium courgette, chopped
½ medium red bell pepper, seeded and chopped
¼ medium red onion, peeled

and sliced
1 tablespoon coconut oil
1 teaspoon dried oregano
½ teaspoon garlic powder
¼ teaspoon dried thyme

1. Place all ingredients into a large mixing bowl and toss until the coconut oil coats the meat and vegetables. Pour the contents of the bowl into the air fryer basket. 2. Adjust the temperature to (190ºC and air fry for 15 minutes. 3. Shake the basket halfway through the cooking time to redistribute the food. Serve immediately.

# Potato–Crusted Chicken

**Prep time: 15 minutes | Cook time: 22 to 25 minutes**

**| Serves 4**

60 g buttermilk
1 large egg, beaten
180 g instant potato flakes
20 g grated Parmesan cheese
1 teaspoon salt
½ teaspoon freshly ground

black pepper
2 whole boneless, skinless chicken breasts (about 450 g each), halved
1 to 2 tablespoons oil

1. In a shallow bowl, whisk the buttermilk and egg until blended. In another shallow bowl, stir together the potato flakes, cheese, salt, and pepper. 2. One at a time, dip the chicken pieces in the buttermilk mixture and the potato flake mixture, coating thoroughly. 3. Preheat the air fryer to 200ºC. Line the air fryer basket with parchment paper. 4. Place the coated chicken on the parchment and spritz with oil. 5. Cook for 15 minutes. Flip the chicken, spritz it with oil, and cook for 7 to 10 minutes more until the outside is crispy and the inside is no longer pink.

# Crunchy Chicken Tenders

**Prep time: 5 minutes | Cook time: 12 minutes |**

**Serves 4**

1 egg
60 ml unsweetened almond milk
15 g whole wheat flour
15 g whole wheat bread crumbs
½ teaspoon salt

½ teaspoon black pepper
½ teaspoon dried thyme
½ teaspoon dried sage
½ teaspoon garlic powder
450 g chicken tenderloins
1 lemon, quartered

1. Preheat the air fryer to 184ºC. 2. In a shallow bowl, beat together the egg and almond milk until frothy. 3. In a separate shallow bowl, whisk together the flour, bread crumbs, salt, pepper, thyme, sage, and garlic powder. 4. Dip each chicken tenderloin into the egg mixture, then into the bread crumb mixture, coating the outside with the crumbs. Place the breaded chicken tenderloins into the bottom of the air fryer basket in an even layer, making sure that they don't touch each other. 5. Cook for 6 minutes, then turn and cook for an additional 5 to 6 minutes. Serve with lemon slices.

# Smoky Chicken Leg Quarters

**Prep time: 30 minutes | Cook time: 23 to 27 minutes**

**| Serves 6**

120 ml avocado oil
2 teaspoons smoked paprika
1 teaspoon sea salt
1 teaspoon garlic powder
½ teaspoon dried rosemary

½ teaspoon dried thyme
½ teaspoon freshly ground black pepper
900 g bone-in, skin-on chicken leg quarters

1. In a blender or small bowl, combine the avocado oil, smoked paprika, salt, garlic powder, rosemary, thyme, and black pepper. 2. Place the chicken in a shallow dish or large zip-top bag. Pour the marinade over the chicken, making sure all the legs are coated. Cover and marinate for at least 2 hours or overnight. 3. Place the chicken in a single layer in the air fryer basket, working in batches if necessary. Set the air fryer to 200ºC and air fry for 15 minutes. Flip the chicken legs, then reduce the temperature to 180ºC. . Cook for 8 to 12 minutes more, until an instant-read thermometer reads 70ºC when inserted into the thickest piece of chicken. 4. Allow to rest for 5 to 10 minutes before serving.

# Brazilian Tempero Baiano Chicken Drumsticks

**Prep time: 30 minutes | Cook time: 20 minutes | Serves 4**

1 teaspoon cumin seeds

1 teaspoon dried oregano

1 teaspoon dried parsley

1 teaspoon ground turmeric

½ teaspoon coriander seeds

1 teaspoon kosher salt

½ teaspoon black peppercorns

½ teaspoon cayenne pepper

60 ml fresh lime juice

2 tablespoons olive oil

680 g chicken drumsticks

1. In a clean coffee grinder or spice mill, combine the cumin, oregano, parsley, turmeric, coriander seeds, salt, peppercorns, and cayenne. Process until finely ground. 2. In a small bowl, combine the ground spices with the lime juice and oil. Place the chicken in a resealable plastic bag. Add the marinade, seal, and massage until the chicken is well coated. Marinate at room temperature for 30 minutes or in the refrigerator for up to 24 hours. 3. When you are ready to cook, place the drumsticks skin side up in the air fryer basket. Set the air fryer to 200°C for 20 to 25 minutes, turning the legs halfway through the cooking time. Use a meat thermometer to ensure that the chicken has reached an internal temperature of 76°C. 4. Serve with plenty of napkins.

# Cranberry Curry Chicken

**Prep time: 12 minutes | Cook time: 18 minutes | Serves 4**

3 (140 g) low-sodium boneless, skinless chicken breasts, cut into

1½-inch cubes

2 teaspoons olive oil

2 tablespoons cornflour

1 tablespoon curry powder

1 tart apple, chopped

120 ml low-sodium chicken broth

60 g dried cranberries

2 tablespoons freshly squeezed orange juice

Brown rice, cooked (optional)

1. Preheat the air fryer to 196°C. 2. In a medium bowl, mix the chicken and olive oil. Sprinkle with the cornflour and curry powder. Toss to coat. Stir in the apple and transfer to a metal pan. Bake in the air fryer for 8 minutes, stirring once during cooking. 3. Add the chicken broth, cranberries, and orange juice. Bake for about 10 minutes more, or until the sauce is slightly thickened and the chicken reaches an internal temperature of 76°C on a meat thermometer. Serve over hot cooked brown rice, if desired.

# Chapter 5 Beef, Pork, and Lamb

# Chapter 5 Beef, Pork, and Lamb

## Simple Beef Mince with Courgette

**Prep time: 5 minutes | Cook time: 12 minutes |**
**Serves 4**

| | |
|---|---|
| 680 g beef mince | 1 teaspoon dried basil |
| 450 g chopped courgette | 1 teaspoon dried rosemary |
| 2 tablespoons extra-virgin olive oil | 2 tablespoons fresh chives, chopped |
| 1 teaspoon dried oregano | |

1. Preheat the air fryer to 200ºC. 2. In a large bowl, combine all the ingredients, except for the chives, until well blended. 3. Place the beef and courgette mixture in the baking tray. Air fry for 12 minutes, or until the beef is browned and the courgette is tender. 4. Divide the beef and courgette mixture among four serving dishes. Top with fresh chives and serve hot.

## Barbecue Ribs

**Prep time: 5 minutes | Cook time: 30 minutes |**
**Serves 4**

| | |
|---|---|
| 1 (900 g) rack baby back ribs | Salt and freshly ground black pepper, to taste |
| 1 teaspoon onion granules | Cooking oil spray |
| 1 teaspoon garlic powder | 120 ml barbecue sauce |
| 1 teaspoon light brown sugar | |
| 1 teaspoon dried oregano | |

1. Use a sharp knife to remove the thin membrane from the back of the ribs. Cut the rack in half, or as needed, so the ribs fit in the air fryer basket. The best way to do this is to cut the ribs into 4- or 5-rib sections. 2. In a small bowl, stir together the onion granules, garlic powder, brown sugar, and oregano and season with salt and pepper. Rub the spice seasoning onto the front and back of the ribs. 3. Cover the ribs with plastic wrap or foil and let sit at room temperature for 30 minutes. 4. Insert the crisper plate into the basket and the basket into the unit. Preheat the unit by selecting AIR ROAST, setting the temperature to 180ºC, and setting the time to 3 minutes. Select START/STOP to begin. 5. Once the unit is preheated, spray the crisper plate with cooking oil. Place the ribs into the basket. It is okay to stack them. 6. Select AIR ROAST, set the temperature to 180ºC, and set the time to 30 minutes. Select START/STOP to begin. 7. After 15 minutes, flip the ribs. Resume cooking for 15 minutes, or until a food thermometer registers 88ºC. 8. When the cooking is complete, transfer the ribs to a serving dish. Drizzle the ribs with the barbecue sauce and serve.

## Garlic Butter Steak Bites

**Prep time: 5 minutes | Cook time: 16 minutes |**
**Serves 3**

| | |
|---|---|
| Oil, for spraying | sauce |
| 450 g boneless steak, cut into 1-inch pieces | ½ teaspoon granulated garlic |
| 2 tablespoons olive oil | ½ teaspoon salt |
| 1 teaspoon Worcestershire | ¼ teaspoon freshly ground black pepper |

1. Preheat the air fryer to 200ºC. Line the air fryer basket with parchment and spray lightly with oil. 2. In a medium bowl, combine the steak, olive oil, Worcestershire sauce, garlic, salt, and black pepper and toss until evenly coated. 3. Place the steak in a single layer in the prepared basket. You may have to work in batches, depending on the size of your air fryer. 4. Cook for 10 to 16 minutes, flipping every 3 to 4 minutes. The total cooking time will depend on the thickness of the meat and your preferred doneness. If you want it well done, it may take up to 5 additional minutes.

## Chorizo and Beef Burger

**Prep time: 10 minutes | Cook time: 15 minutes |**
**Serves 4**

| | |
|---|---|
| 340 g 80/20 beef mince | chopped |
| 110 g Mexican-style chorizo crumb | 2 teaspoons chili powder |
| 60 g chopped onion | 1 teaspoon minced garlic |
| 5 slices pickled jalapeños, | ¼ teaspoon cumin |

1. In a large bowl, mix all ingredients. Divide the mixture into four sections and form them into burger patties. 2. Place burger patties into the air fryer basket, working in batches if necessary. 3. Adjust the temperature to 190ºC and air fry for 15 minutes. 4. Flip the patties halfway through the cooking time. Serve warm.

# Greek Stuffed Fillet

**Prep time: 10 minutes | Cook time: 10 minutes | Serves 4**

680 g venison or beef fillet, pounded to ¼ inch thick
3 teaspoons fine sea salt
1 teaspoon ground black pepper
60 g creamy goat cheese
120 g crumbled feta cheese (about 60 g)
60 g finely chopped onions

2 cloves garlic, minced
For Garnish/Serving (Optional):
Yellow/American mustard
Halved cherry tomatoes
Extra-virgin olive oil
Sprigs of fresh rosemary
Lavender flowers

1. Spray the air fryer basket with avocado oil. Preheat the air fryer to 200°C. 2. Season the fillet on all sides with the salt and pepper. 3. In a medium-sized mixing bowl, combine the goat cheese, feta, onions, and garlic. Place the mixture in the center of the tenderloin. Starting at the end closest to you, tightly roll the tenderloin like a jelly roll. Tie the rolled tenderloin tightly with kitchen twine. 4. Place the meat in the air fryer basket and air fry for 5 minutes. Flip the meat over and cook for another 5 minutes, or until the internal temperature reaches 57°C for medium-rare. 5. To serve, smear a line of yellow mustard on a platter, then place the meat next to it and add halved cherry tomatoes on the side, if desired. Drizzle with olive oil and garnish with rosemary sprigs and lavender flowers, if desired. 6. Best served fresh. Store leftovers in an airtight container in the fridge for 3 days. Reheat in a preheated 180°C air fryer for 4 minutes, or until heated through.

# Chuck Kebab with Rocket

**Prep time: 30 minutes | Cook time: 25 minutes | Serves 4**

120 g leeks, chopped
2 garlic cloves, smashed
900 g beef mince
Salt, to taste
¼ teaspoon ground black pepper, or more to taste
1 teaspoon cayenne pepper

½ teaspoon ground sumac
3 saffron threads
2 tablespoons loosely packed fresh flat-leaf parsley leaves
4 tablespoons tahini sauce
110 g baby rocket
1 tomato, cut into slices

1. In a bowl, mix the chopped leeks, garlic, beef mince, and spices; knead with your hands until everything is well incorporated. 2. Now, mound the beef mixture around a wooden skewer into a pointed-ended sausage. 3. Cook in the preheated air fryer at 180°C for 25 minutes. Serve your kebab with the tahini sauce, baby rocket and tomato. Enjoy!

# Goat Cheese–Stuffed Bavette Steak

**Prep time: 10 minutes | Cook time: 14 minutes | Serves 6**

450 g bavette or skirt steak
1 tablespoon avocado oil
½ teaspoon sea salt
½ teaspoon garlic powder

¼ teaspoon freshly ground black pepper
60 g goat cheese, crumbled
235 g baby spinach, chopped

1. Place the steak in a large zip-top bag or between two pieces of plastic wrap. Using a meat mallet or heavy-bottomed skillet, pound the steak to an even ¼-inch thickness. 2. Brush both sides of the steak with the avocado oil. 3. Mix the salt, garlic powder, and pepper in a small dish. Sprinkle this mixture over both sides of the steak. 4. Sprinkle the goat cheese over top, and top that with the spinach. 5. Starting at one of the long sides, roll the steak up tightly. Tie the rolled steak with kitchen string at 3-inch intervals. 6. Set the air fryer to 200°C. Place the steak roll-up in the air fryer basket. Air fry for 7 minutes. Flip the steak and cook for an additional 7 minutes, until an instant-read thermometer reads 49°C for medium-rare (adjust the cooking time for your desired doneness).

# Mojito Lamb Chops

**Prep time: 30 minutes | Cook time: 5 minutes | Serves 2**

Marinade:
2 teaspoons grated lime zest
120 ml lime juice
60 ml avocado oil
60 g chopped fresh mint leaves
4 cloves garlic, roughly chopped
2 teaspoons fine sea salt

½ teaspoon ground black pepper
4 (1-inch-thick) lamb chops
Sprigs of fresh mint, for garnish (optional)
Lime slices, for serving (optional)

1. Make the marinade: Place all the ingredients for the marinade in a food processor or blender and purée until mostly smooth with a few small chunks. Transfer half of the marinade to a shallow dish and set the other half aside for serving. Add the lamb to the shallow dish, cover, and place in the refrigerator to marinate for at least 2 hours or overnight. 2. Spray the air fryer basket with avocado oil. Preheat the air fryer to 200°C. 3. Remove the chops from the marinade and place them in the air fryer basket. Air fry for 5 minutes, or until the internal temperature reaches 64°C for medium doneness. 4. Allow the chops to rest for 10 minutes before serving with the rest of the marinade as a sauce. Garnish with fresh mint leaves and serve with lime slices, if desired. Best served fresh.

# Ham Hock Mac and Cheese

**Prep time: 20 minutes | Cook time: 25 minutes | Serves 4**

2 large eggs, beaten
475 g cottage cheese, full-fat or low-fat
475 g grated sharp Cheddar cheese, divided
235 ml sour cream
½ teaspoon salt
1 teaspoon freshly ground black pepper
475 g uncooked elbow macaroni
2 ham hocks (about 310 g each), meat removed and diced
1 to 2 tablespoons oil

1. In a large bowl, stir together the eggs, cottage cheese, 235 ml of the Cheddar cheese, sour cream, salt, and pepper. 2. Stir in the macaroni and the diced meat. 3. Preheat the air fryer to 180ºC. Spritz a baking tray with oil. 4. Pour the macaroni mixture into the prepared pan, making sure all noodles are covered with sauce. 5. Cook for 12 minutes. Stir in the remaining 235 ml of Cheddar cheese, making sure all the noodles are covered with sauce. Cook for 13 minutes more, until the noodles are tender. Let rest for 5 minutes before serving.

# Parmesan–Crusted Steak

**Prep time: 30 minutes | Cook time: 12 minutes | Serves 6**

120 ml (1 stick) unsalted butter, at room temperature
235 g finely grated Parmesan cheese
30 g finely ground blanched
almond flour
680 g sirloin steak
Sea salt and freshly ground black pepper, to taste

1. Place the butter, Parmesan cheese, and almond flour in a food processor. Process until smooth. Transfer to a sheet of parchment paper and form into a log. Wrap tightly in plastic wrap. Freeze for 45 minutes or refrigerate for at least 4 hours. 2. While the butter is chilling, season the steak liberally with salt and pepper. Let the steak rest at room temperature for about 45 minutes. 3. Place the grill pan or basket in your air fryer, set it to 200ºC, and let it preheat for 5 minutes. 4. Working in batches, if necessary, place the steak on the grill pan and air fry for 4 minutes. Flip and cook for 3 minutes more, until the steak is brown on both sides. 5. Remove the steak from the air fryer and arrange an equal amount of the Parmesan butter on top of each steak. Return the steak to the air fryer and continue cooking for another 5 minutes, until an instant-read thermometer reads 49ºC for medium-rare and the crust is golden brown (or to your desired doneness). 6. Transfer the cooked steak to a plate; let rest for 10 minutes before serving.

# Pork Loin with Aloha Salsa

**Prep time: 20 minutes | Cook time: 7 to 9 minutes | Serves 4**

Aloha Salsa:
235 g fresh pineapple, chopped in small pieces
60 g red onion, finely chopped
60 g green or red pepper, chopped
½ teaspoon ground cinnamon
1 teaspoon reduced-salt soy sauce
⅛ teaspoon crushed red pepper
⅛ teaspoon ground black pepper
2 eggs
2 tablespoons milk
30 g flour
30 g panko bread crumbs
4 teaspoons sesame seeds
450 g boneless, thin pork loin or tenderloin (⅜- to ½-inch thick)
Pepper and salt
30 g cornflour
Oil for misting or cooking spray

1. In a medium bowl, stir together all ingredients for salsa. Cover and refrigerate while cooking pork. 2. Preheat the air fryer to 200ºC. 3. Beat together eggs and milk in shallow dish. 4. In another shallow dish, mix together the flour, panko, and sesame seeds. 5. Sprinkle pork with pepper and salt to taste. 6. Dip pork in cornflour, egg mixture, and then panko coating. Spray both sides with oil or cooking spray. 7. Cook pork for 3 minutes. Turn pork over, spraying both sides, and continue cooking for 4 to 6 minutes or until well done. 8. Serve fried cutlets with salsa on the side.

# Indian Mint and Chile Kebabs

**Prep time: 30 minutes | Cook time: 15 minutes | Serves 4**

450 g lamb mince
120 g finely minced onion
60 g chopped fresh mint
60 g chopped fresh coriander
1 tablespoon minced garlic
½ teaspoon ground turmeric
½ teaspoon cayenne pepper
¼ teaspoon ground cardamom
¼ teaspoon ground cinnamon
1 teaspoon coarse or flaky salt

1. In the bowl of a stand mixer fitted with the paddle attachment, combine the lamb, onion, mint, coriander, garlic, turmeric, cayenne, cardamom, cinnamon, and salt. Mix on low speed until you have a sticky mess of spiced meat. If you have time, let the mixture stand at room temperature for 30 minutes (or cover and refrigerate for up to a day or two, until you're ready to make the kebabs). 2. Divide the meat into eight equal portions. Form each into a long sausage shape. Place the kebabs in a single layer in the air fryer basket. Set the air fryer to 180ºC for 10 minutes. Increase the air fryer temperature to 200ºC and cook for 3 to 4 minutes more to brown the kebabs. Use a meat thermometer to ensure the kebabs have reached an internal temperature of 72ºC (medium).

# Italian Pork Loin

**Prep time: 30 minutes | Cook time: 16 minutes | Serves 3**

1 teaspoon sea salt

½ teaspoon black pepper, freshly cracked

60 ml red wine

2 tablespoons mustard

2 garlic cloves, minced

450 g pork loin joint

1 tablespoon Italian herb seasoning blend

1. In a ceramic bowl, mix the salt, black pepper, red wine, mustard, and garlic. Add the pork loin and let it marinate at least 30 minutes. 2. Spritz the sides and bottom of the air fryer basket with nonstick cooking spray. 3. Place the pork loin in the basket; sprinkle with the Italian herb seasoning blend. Cook the pork loin at 190°C for 10 minutes. Flip halfway through, spraying with cooking oil and cook for 5 to 6 minutes more. Serve immediately.

# Steak with Bell Pepper

**Prep time: 30 minutes | Cook time: 20 to 23 minutes | Serves 6**

60 ml avocado oil

60 g freshly squeezed lime juice

2 teaspoons minced garlic

1 tablespoon chili powder

½ teaspoon ground cumin

Sea salt and freshly ground black pepper, to taste

450 g top rump steak or bavette

or skirt steak, thinly sliced against the grain

1 red pepper, cored, seeded, and cut into ½-inch slices

1 green pepper, cored, seeded, and cut into ½-inch slices

1 large onion, sliced

1. In a small bowl or blender, combine the avocado oil, lime juice, garlic, chili powder, cumin, and salt and pepper to taste. 2. Place the sliced steak in a zip-top bag or shallow dish. Place the peppers and onion in a separate zip-top bag or dish. Pour half the marinade over the steak and the other half over the vegetables. Seal both bags and let the steak and vegetables marinate in the refrigerator for at least 1 hour or up to 4 hours. 3. Line the air fryer basket with an air fryer liner or aluminum foil. Remove the vegetables from their bag or dish and shake off any excess marinade. Set the air fryer to 200°C. Place the vegetables in the air fryer basket and cook for 13 minutes. 4. Remove the steak from its bag or dish and shake off any excess marinade. Place the steak on top of the vegetables in the air fryer, and cook for 7 to 10 minutes or until an instant-read thermometer reads 49°C for medium-rare (or cook to your desired doneness). 5. Serve with desired fixings, such as keto tortillas, lettuce, sour cream, avocado slices, shredded Cheddar cheese, and coriander.

# Rosemary Roast Beef

**Prep time: 30 minutes | Cook time: 30 to 35 minutes | Serves 8**

1 (900 g) beef roasting joint, tied with kitchen string

Sea salt and freshly ground black pepper, to taste

2 teaspoons minced garlic

2 tablespoons finely chopped fresh rosemary

60 ml avocado oil

1. Season the roast generously with salt and pepper. 2. In a small bowl, whisk together the garlic, rosemary, and avocado oil. Rub this all over the roast. Cover loosely with aluminum foil or plastic wrap and refrigerate for at least 12 hours or up to 2 days. 3. Remove the roast from the refrigerator and allow to sit at room temperature for about 1 hour. 4. Set the air fryer to 160°C. Place the roast in the air fryer basket and roast for 15 minutes. Flip the roast and cook for 15 to 20 minutes more, until the meat is browned and an instant-read thermometer reads 49°C at the thickest part (for medium-rare). 5. Transfer the meat to a cutting board, and let it rest for 15 minutes before thinly slicing and serving.

# Asian Glazed Meatballs

**Prep time: 15 minutes | Cook time: 10 minutes per batch | Serves 4 to 6**

1 large shallot, finely chopped

2 cloves garlic, minced

1 tablespoon grated fresh ginger

2 teaspoons fresh thyme, finely chopped

355 g brown mushrooms, very finely chopped (a food processor works well here)

2 tablespoons soy sauce

Freshly ground black pepper, to

taste

450 g beef mince

230 g pork mince

3 egg yolks

235 ml Thai sweet chili sauce (spring roll sauce)

60 g toasted sesame seeds

2 spring onion spring onions, sliced

1. Combine the shallot, garlic, ginger, thyme, mushrooms, soy sauce, freshly ground black pepper, beef and pork mince, and egg yolks in a bowl and mix the ingredients together. Gently shape the mixture into 24 balls, about the size of a golf ball. 2. Preheat the air fryer to 190°C. 3. Working in batches, air fry the meatballs for 8 minutes, turning the meatballs over halfway through the cooking time. Drizzle some of the Thai sweet chili sauce on top of each meatball and return the basket to the air fryer, air frying for another 2 minutes. Reserve the remaining Thai sweet chili sauce for serving. 4. As soon as the meatballs are done, sprinkle with toasted sesame seeds and transfer them to a serving platter. Scatter the spring onion spring onions around and serve warm.

# BBQ Pork Steaks

**Prep time: 5 minutes | Cook time: 15 minutes |**
**Serves 4**

| | |
|---|---|
| 4 pork steaks | 1 teaspoon soy sauce |
| 1 tablespoon Cajun seasoning | 96 g brown sugar |
| 2 tablespoons BBQ sauce | 120 ml ketchup |
| 1 tablespoon vinegar | |

1. Preheat the air fryer to 140ºC. 2. Sprinkle pork steaks with Cajun seasoning. 3. Combine remaining ingredients and brush onto steaks. 4. Add coated steaks to air fryer. Air fry 15 minutes until just browned. 5. Serve immediately.

# Pork Medallions with Endive Salad

**Prep time: 25 minutes | Cook time: 7 minutes |**
**Serves 4**

| | |
|---|---|
| 1 (230 g) pork tenderloin | honey or maple syrup) |
| Salt and freshly ground black pepper, to taste | 1 tablespoon Dijon mustard |
| 30 g flour | juice of ½ lemon |
| 2 eggs, lightly beaten | 2 tablespoons chopped chervil or flat-leaf parsley |
| 180 g finely crushed crackers | salt and freshly ground black pepper |
| 1 teaspoon paprika | |
| 1 teaspoon mustard powder | 120 ml extra-virgin olive oil |
| 1 teaspoon garlic powder | Endive Salad: |
| 1 teaspoon dried thyme | 1 heart romaine lettuce, torn into large pieces |
| 1 teaspoon salt | |
| vegetable or rapeseed oil, in spray bottle | 2 heads endive, sliced |
| | 120 g cherry tomatoes, halved |
| Vinaigrette: | 85 g fresh Mozzarella, diced |
| 60 ml white balsamic vinegar | Salt and freshly ground black pepper, to taste |
| 2 tablespoons agave syrup (or | |

1. Slice the pork tenderloin into 1-inch slices. Using a meat pounder, pound the pork slices into thin ½-inch medallions. Generously season the pork with salt and freshly ground black pepper on both sides. 2. Set up a dredging station using three shallow dishes. Put the flour in one dish and the beaten eggs in a second dish. Combine the crushed crackers, paprika, mustard powder, garlic powder, thyme and salt in a third dish. 3. Preheat the air fryer to 200ºC. 4. Dredge the pork medallions in flour first and then into the beaten egg. Let the excess egg drip off and coat both sides of the medallions with the cracker crumb mixture. Spray both sides of the coated medallions with vegetable or rapeseed oil. 5. Air fry the medallions in two batches at 200ºC for 5 minutes. Once you have air-fried all the medallions, flip them all over and return the first batch of medallions back into the air fryer on top of the second batch. Air fry at 200ºC for an additional 2 minutes. 6. While the medallions are cooking, make the salad and dressing. Whisk the white balsamic vinegar, agave syrup, Dijon mustard, lemon juice, chervil, salt and pepper together in a small bowl. Whisk in the olive oil slowly until combined and thickened. 7. Combine the romaine lettuce, endive, cherry tomatoes, and Mozzarella cheese in a large salad bowl. Drizzle the dressing over the vegetables and toss to combine. Season with salt and freshly ground black pepper. 8. Serve the pork medallions warm on or beside the salad.

# Pork Chops with Caramelized Onions

**Prep time: 20 minutes | Cook time: 23 to 34 minutes**
**| Serves 4**

| | |
|---|---|
| 4 bone-in pork chops (230 g each) | divided |
| | 1 brown onion, thinly sliced |
| 1 to 2 tablespoons oil | 1 green pepper, thinly sliced |
| 2 tablespoons Cajun seasoning, | 2 tablespoons light brown sugar |

1. Spritz the pork chops with oil. Sprinkle 1 tablespoon of Cajun seasoning on one side of the chops. 2. Preheat the air fryer to 200ºC. Line the air fryer basket with parchment paper and spritz the parchment with oil. 3. Place 2 pork chops, spice-side up, on the paper. 4. Cook for 4 minutes. Flip the chops, sprinkle with the remaining 1 tablespoon of Cajun seasoning, and cook for 4 to 8 minutes more until the internal temperature reaches 64ºC, depending on the chops' thickness. Remove and keep warm while you cook the remaining 2 chops. Set the chops aside. 5. In a baking tray, combine the onion, pepper, and brown sugar, stirring until the vegetables are coated. Place the pan in the air fryer basket and cook for 4 minutes. 6. Stir the vegetables. Cook for 3 to 6 minutes more to your desired doneness. Spoon the vegetable mixture over the chops to serve.

# Mexican Pork Chops

**Prep time: 5 minutes | Cook time: 15 minutes |**
**Serves 2**

| | |
|---|---|
| ¼ teaspoon dried oregano | 2 (110 g) boneless pork chops |
| 1½ teaspoons taco seasoning or fajita seasoning mix | 2 tablespoons unsalted butter, divided |

1. Preheat the air fryer to 200ºC. 2. Combine the dried oregano and taco seasoning in a small bowl and rub the mixture into the pork chops. Brush the chops with 1 tablespoon butter. 3. In the air fryer, air fry the chops for 15 minutes, turning them over halfway through to air fry on the other side. 4. When the chops are a brown color, check the internal temperature has reached 64ºC and remove from the air fryer. Serve with a garnish of remaining butter.

# Italian Sausage Links

**Prep time: 10 minutes | Cook time: 24 minutes |**
**Serves 4**

1 pepper (any color), sliced
1 medium onion, sliced
1 tablespoon avocado oil
1 teaspoon Italian seasoning

Sea salt and freshly ground
black pepper, to taste
450 g Italian-seasoned sausage
links

1. Place the pepper and onion in a medium bowl, and toss with the avocado oil, Italian seasoning, and salt and pepper to taste. 2. Set the air fryer to 200ºC. Put the vegetables in the air fryer basket and cook for 12 minutes. 3. Push the vegetables to the side of the basket and arrange the sausage links in the bottom of the basket in a single layer. Spoon the vegetables over the sausages. Cook for 12 minutes, tossing halfway through, until an instant-read thermometer inserted into the sausage reads 72ºC.

# Rack of Lamb with Pistachio Crust

**Prep time: 10 minutes | Cook time: 19 minutes |**
**Serves 2**

120 g finely chopped pistachios
3 tablespoons panko bread
crumbs
1 teaspoon chopped fresh
rosemary
2 teaspoons chopped fresh
oregano

Salt and freshly ground black
pepper, to taste
1 tablespoon olive oil
1 rack of lamb, bones trimmed
of fat and frenched
1 tablespoon Dijon mustard

1. Preheat the air fryer to 190ºC. 2. Combine the pistachios, bread crumbs, rosemary, oregano, salt and pepper in a small bowl. (This is a good job for your food processor if you have one.) Drizzle in the olive oil and stir to combine. 3. Season the rack of lamb with salt and pepper on all sides and transfer it to the air fryer basket with the fat side facing up. Air fry the lamb for 12 minutes. Remove the lamb from the air fryer and brush the fat side of the lamb rack with the Dijon mustard. Coat the rack with the pistachio mixture, pressing the bread crumbs onto the lamb with your hands and rolling the bottom of the rack in any of the crumbs that fall off. 4. Return the rack of lamb to the air fryer and air fry for another 3 to 7 minutes or until an instant read thermometer reads 60ºC for medium. Add or subtract a couple of minutes for lamb that is more or less well cooked. (Your time will vary depending on how big the rack of lamb is.) 5. Let the lamb rest for at least 5 minutes. Then, slice into chops and serve.

# Marinated Steak Tips with Mushrooms

**Prep time: 30 minutes | Cook time: 10 minutes |**
**Serves 4**

680 g rump steak, trimmed and
cut into 1-inch pieces
230 g brown mushrooms,
halved
60 ml Worcestershire sauce
1 tablespoon Dijon mustard

1 tablespoon olive oil
1 teaspoon paprika
1 teaspoon crushed red pepper
flakes
2 tablespoons chopped fresh
parsley (optional)

1. Place the beef and mushrooms in a gallon-size resealable bag. In a small bowl, whisk together the Worcestershire, mustard, olive oil, paprika, and red pepper flakes. Pour the marinade into the bag and massage gently to ensure the beef and mushrooms are evenly coated. Seal the bag and refrigerate for at least 4 hours, preferably overnight. Remove from the refrigerator 30 minutes before cooking. 2. Preheat the air fryer to 200ºC. 3. Drain and discard the marinade. Arrange the steak and mushrooms in the air fryer basket. Air fry for 10 minutes, pausing halfway through the baking time to shake the basket. Transfer to a serving plate and top with the parsley, if desired.

# Honey–Baked Pork Loin

**Prep time: 30 minutes | Cook time: 22 to 25 minutes**
**| Serves 6**

60 ml honey
60 g freshly squeezed lemon
juice
2 tablespoons soy sauce

1 teaspoon garlic powder
1 (900 g) pork loin
2 tablespoons vegetable oil

1. In a medium bowl, whisk together the honey, lemon juice, soy sauce, and garlic powder. Reserve half of the mixture for basting during cooking. 2. Cut 5 slits in the pork loin and transfer it to a resealable bag. Add the remaining honey mixture. Seal the bag and refrigerate to marinate for at least 2 hours. 3. Preheat the air fryer to 200ºC. Line the air fryer basket with parchment paper. 4. Remove the pork from the marinade, and place it on the parchment. Spritz with oil, then baste with the reserved marinade. 5. Cook for 15 minutes. Flip the pork, baste with more marinade and spritz with oil again. Cook for 7 to 10 minutes more until the internal temperature reaches 64ºC. Let rest for 5 minutes before serving.

# Pork Tenderloin with Avocado Lime Sauce

**Prep time: 30 minutes | Cook time: 15 minutes | Serves 4**

Marinade:

120 ml lime juice

Grated zest of 1 lime

2 teaspoons stevia glycerite, or ¼ teaspoon liquid stevia

3 cloves garlic, minced

1½ teaspoons fine sea salt

1 teaspoon chili powder, or more for more heat

1 teaspoon smoked paprika

450 g pork tenderloin

Avocado Lime Sauce:

1 medium-sized ripe avocado, roughly chopped

120 ml full-fat sour cream (or coconut cream for dairy-free)

Grated zest of 1 lime

Juice of 1 lime

2 cloves garlic, roughly chopped

½ teaspoon fine sea salt

¼ teaspoon ground black pepper

Chopped fresh coriander leaves, for garnish

Lime slices, for serving

Pico de gallo or salsa, for serving

1. In a medium-sized casserole dish, stir together all the marinade ingredients until well combined. Add the tenderloin and coat it well in the marinade. Cover and place in the fridge to marinate for 2 hours or overnight. 2. Spray the air fryer basket with avocado oil. Preheat the air fryer to 200°C. 3. Remove the pork from the marinade and place it in the air fryer basket. Air fry for 13 to 15 minutes, until the internal temperature of the pork is 64°C, flipping after 7 minutes. Remove the pork from the air fryer and place it on a cutting board. Allow it to rest for 8 to 10 minutes, then cut it into ½-inch-thick slices. 4. While the pork cooks, make the avocado lime sauce: Place all the sauce ingredients in a food processor and purée until smooth. Taste and adjust the seasoning to your liking. 5. Place the pork slices on a serving platter and spoon the avocado lime sauce on top. Garnish with coriander leaves and serve with lime slices and pico de gallo. 6. Store leftovers in an airtight container in the fridge for up to 4 days. Reheat in a preheated 200°C air fryer for 5 minutes, or until heated through.

# Chapter 6 Fish and Seafood

# Chapter 6 Fish and Seafood

## Crab Legs

**Prep time: 5 minutes | Cook time: 15 minutes |**
**Serves 4**

60 g salted butter, melted and
divided
1.4 kg crab legs

¼ teaspoon garlic powder
Juice of ½ medium lemon

1. In a large bowl, drizzle 2 tablespoons butter over crab legs. Place crab legs into the air fryer basket. 2. Adjust the temperature to 200ºC and air fry for 15 minutes. 3. Shake the air fryer basket to toss the crab legs halfway through the cooking time. 4. In a small bowl, mix remaining butter, garlic powder, and lemon juice. 5. To serve, crack open crab legs and remove meat. Dip in lemon butter.

## Crab Cakes with Mango Mayo

**Prep time: 25 minutes | Cook time: 15 minutes |**
**Serves 4**

Crab Cakes:
235 g chopped red onion
8 g fresh coriander leaves
1 small serrano chilli or
jalapeño, seeded and quartered
230 g lump crab meat
1 large egg
1 tablespoon mayonnaise
1 tablespoon whole-grain
mustard
2 teaspoons minced fresh ginger
½ teaspoon ground cumin

½ teaspoon ground coriander
¼ teaspoon kosher or coarse sea
salt
2 tablespoons fresh lemon juice
45 g panko bread crumbs
Vegetable oil spray
Mango Mayo:
80 g diced fresh mango
115 g mayonnaise
½ teaspoon grated lime zest
2 teaspoons fresh lime juice
Pinch of cayenne pepper

1. For the crab cakes: Combine the onion, coriander leaves, and serrano in a food processor. Pulse until minced. 2. In a large bowl, combine the minced vegetable mixture with the crab meat, egg, mayonnaise, mustard, ginger, cumin, ground coriander, and salt. Add the lemon juice and mix gently until thoroughly combined. Add 60 g of the bread crumbs. Mix gently again until well blended. 3. Form into four evenly sized patties. Put the remaining 30 g bread crumbs in a shallow bowl and press both sides of each patty into the bread crumbs. 4. Arrange the patties in the air fryer basket. Spray with vegetable oil spray. Set the air fryer to 190ºC for 15 minutes, turning and spraying other side of the patties with vegetable oil spray halfway through the cooking time, until the crab cakes are golden brown and crisp. 5. Meanwhile, for the mayonnaise: In a blender, combine the mango, mayonnaise, lime zest, lime juice, and cayenne. Blend until smooth. 6. Serve the crab cakes warm, with the mango mayo.

## Sole Fillets

**Prep time: 10 minutes | Cook time: 5 to 8 minutes |**
**Serves 4**

1 egg white
1 tablespoon water
30 g panko breadcrumbs
2 tablespoons extra-light virgin
olive oil

4 sole fillets, 110 g each
Salt and pepper, to taste
Olive or vegetable oil for
misting or cooking spray

1. Preheat the air fryer to 390ºF (200ºC). 2. Beat together egg white and water in shallow dish. 3. In another shallow dish, mix panko crumbs and oil until well combined and crumbly (best done by hand). 4. Season sole fillets with salt and pepper to taste. Dip each fillet into egg mixture and then roll in panko crumbs, pressing in crumbs so that fish is nicely coated. 5. Spray the air fryer basket with nonstick cooking spray and add fillets. Air fry at 200ºC for 3 minutes. 6. Spray fish fillets but do not turn. Cook 2 to 5 minutes longer or until golden brown and crispy. Using a spatula, carefully remove fish from basket and serve.

## Simple Buttery Cod

**Prep time: 5 minutes | Cook time: 8 minutes | Serves 2**

2 cod fillets, 110 g each
2 tablespoons salted butter,
melted

1 teaspoon Old Bay seasoning
½ medium lemon, sliced

1. Place cod fillets into a round baking dish. Brush each fillet with butter and sprinkle with Old Bay seasoning. Lay two lemon slices on each fillet. Cover the dish with foil and place into the air fryer basket. 2. Adjust the temperature to 180ºC and bake for 8 minutes. Flip halfway through the cooking time. When cooked, internal temperature should be at least 64ºC. Serve warm.

# Breaded Prawns Tacos

**Prep time: 10 minutes | Cook time: 9 minutes |**
**Makes 8 tacos**

2 large eggs
1 teaspoon prepared yellow mustard
455 g small prawns, peeled, deveined, and tails removed
45 g finely shredded Gouda or Parmesan cheese
80 g pork scratchings ground to

dust
For Serving:
8 large round lettuce leaves
60 ml pico de gallo
20 g shredded purple cabbage
1 lemon, sliced
Guacamole (optional)

1. Preheat the air fryer to 200°C. 2. Crack the eggs into a large bowl, add the mustard, and whisk until well combined. Add the prawns and stir well to coat. 3. In a medium-sized bowl, mix together the cheese and pork scratching dust until well combined. 4. One at a time, roll the coated prawns in the pork scratching dust mixture and use your hands to press it onto each prawns. Spray the coated prawns with avocado oil and place them in the air fryer basket, leaving space between them. 5. Air fry the prawns for 9 minutes, or until cooked through and no longer translucent, flipping after 4 minutes. 6. To serve, place a lettuce leaf on a serving plate, place several prawns on top, and top with 1½ teaspoons each of pico de gallo and purple cabbage. Squeeze some lemon juice on top and serve with guacamole, if desired. 7. Store leftover prawns in an airtight container in the refrigerator for up to 3 days. Reheat in a preheated 200°C air fryer for 5 minutes, or until warmed through.

# Trout Amandine with Lemon Butter Sauce

**Prep time: 20 minutes | Cook time:8 minutes |**
**Serves 4**

Trout Amandine:
65 g toasted almonds
30 g grated Parmesan cheese
1 teaspoon salt
½ teaspoon freshly ground black pepper
2 tablespoons butter, melted
4 trout fillets, or salmon fillets, 110 g each
Cooking spray

Lemon Butter Sauce:
8 tablespoons butter, melted
2 tablespoons freshly squeezed lemon juice
½ teaspoon Worcestershire sauce
½ teaspoon salt
½ teaspoon freshly ground black pepper
¼ teaspoon hot sauce

1. In a blender or food processor, pulse the almonds for 5 to 10 seconds until finely processed. Transfer to a shallow bowl and whisk in the Parmesan cheese, salt, and pepper. Place the melted butter in another shallow bowl. 2. One at a time, dip the fish in

the melted butter, then the almond mixture, coating thoroughly. 3. Preheat the air fryer to 150°C. Line the air fryer basket with baking paper. 4. Place the coated fish on the baking paper and spritz with oil. 5. Bake for 4 minutes. Flip the fish, spritz it with oil, and bake for 4 minutes more until the fish flakes easily with a fork. 6. In a small bowl, whisk the butter, lemon juice, Worcestershire sauce, salt, pepper, and hot sauce until blended. 7. Serve with the fish.

# Almond Pesto Salmon

**Prep time: 5 minutes | Cook time: 12 minutes |**
**Serves 2**

60 g pesto
20 g sliced almonds, roughly chopped
2 (1½-inch-thick) salmon fillets

(about 110 g each)
2 tablespoons unsalted butter, melted

1. In a small bowl, mix pesto and almonds. Set aside. 2. Place fillets into a round baking dish. 3. Brush each fillet with butter and place half of the pesto mixture on the top of each fillet. Place dish into the air fryer basket. 4. Adjust the temperature to 200°C and set the timer for 12 minutes. 5. Salmon will easily flake when fully cooked and reach an internal temperature of at least 64°C. Serve warm.

# Almond–Crusted Fish

**Prep time: 15 minutes | Cook time: 10 minutes |**
**Serves 4**

4 firm white fish fillets, 110g each
25 g breadcrumbs
20 g slivered almonds, crushed
2 tablespoons lemon juice
⅛ teaspoon cayenne

Salt and pepper, to taste
470 g plain flour
1 egg, beaten with 1 tablespoon water
Olive or vegetable oil for misting or cooking spray

1. Split fish fillets lengthwise down the center to create 8 pieces. 2. Mix breadcrumbs and almonds together and set aside. 3. Mix the lemon juice and cayenne together. Brush on all sides of fish. 4. Season fish to taste with salt and pepper. 5. Place the flour on a sheet of wax paper. 6. Roll fillets in flour, dip in egg wash, and roll in the crumb mixture. 7. Mist both sides of fish with oil or cooking spray. 8. Spray the air fryer basket and lay fillets inside. 9. Roast at 200°C for 5 minutes, turn fish over, and cook for an additional 5 minutes or until fish is done and flakes easily.

## Tilapia Sandwiches with Tartar Sauce

**Prep time: 8 minutes | Cook time: 17 minutes | Serves 4**

160 g mayonnaise
2 tablespoons dried minced onion
1 dill pickle spear, finely chopped
2 teaspoons pickle juice
¼ teaspoon salt
⅛ teaspoon freshly ground black pepper

20 g plain flour
1 egg, lightly beaten
100 g panko bread crumbs
2 teaspoons lemon pepper
4 (170 g) tilapia fillets
Olive oil spray
4 soft sub rolls
4 lettuce leaves

1. To make the tartar sauce, in a small bowl, whisk the mayonnaise, dried onion, pickle, pickle juice, salt, and pepper until blended. Refrigerate while you make the fish. 2. Scoop the flour onto a plate; set aside. 3. Put the beaten egg in a medium shallow bowl. 4. On another plate, stir together the panko and lemon pepper. 5. Insert the crisper plate into the basket and the basket into the unit. Preheat the unit to 200ºC. 6. Dredge the tilapia fillets in the flour, in the egg, and press into the panko mixture to coat. 7. Once the unit is preheated, spray the crisper plate with olive oil and place a baking paper liner into the basket. Place the prepared fillets on the liner in a single layer. Lightly spray the fillets with olive oil. 8. cook for 8 minutes, remove the basket, carefully flip the fillets, and spray them with more olive oil. Reinsert the basket to resume cooking. 9. When the cooking is complete, the fillets should be golden and crispy and a food thermometer should register 64ºC. Place each cooked fillet in a sub roll, top with a little bit of tartar sauce and lettuce, and serve.

## Honey–Balsamic Salmon

**Prep time: 5 minutes | Cook time: 8 minutes | Serves 2**

Olive or vegetable oil, for spraying
2 (170 g) salmon fillets
60 ml balsamic vinegar
2 tablespoons honey

2 teaspoons red pepper flakes
2 teaspoons olive oil
½ teaspoon salt
¼ teaspoon freshly ground black pepper

1. Line the air fryer basket with baking paper and spray lightly with oil. 2. Place the salmon in the prepared basket. 3. In a small bowl, whisk together the balsamic vinegar, honey, red pepper flakes, olive oil, salt, and black pepper. Brush the mixture over the salmon. 4. Roast at 200ºC for 7 to 8 minutes, or until the internal temperature reaches 64ºC. Serve immediately.

## Seasoned Tuna Steaks

**Prep time: 5 minutes | Cook time: 9 minutes | Serves 4**

1 teaspoon garlic powder
½ teaspoon salt
¼ teaspoon dried thyme
¼ teaspoon dried oregano

4 tuna steaks
2 tablespoons olive oil
1 lemon, quartered

1. Preheat the air fryer to 190ºC. 2. In a small bowl, whisk together the garlic powder, salt, thyme, and oregano. 3. Coat the tuna steaks with olive oil. Season both sides of each steak with the seasoning blend. Place the steaks in a single layer in the air fryer basket. 4. Roast for 5 minutes, then flip and roast for an additional 3 to 4 minutes.

## Mouthwatering Cod over Creamy Leek Noodles

**Prep time: 10 minutes | Cook time: 24 minutes | Serves 4**

1 small leek, sliced into long thin noodles
120 ml heavy cream
2 cloves garlic, minced
1 teaspoon fine sea salt, divided
4 cod fillets, 110 g each (about 1 inch thick)
½ teaspoon ground black pepper

Coating:
20 g grated Parmesan cheese
2 tablespoons mayonnaise
2 tablespoons unsalted butter, softened
1 tablespoon chopped fresh thyme, or ½ teaspoon dried thyme leaves, plus more for garnish

1. Preheat the air fryer to 180ºC. 2. Place the leek noodles in a casserole dish or a pan that will fit in your air fryer. 3. In a small bowl, stir together the cream, garlic, and ½ teaspoon of the salt. Pour the mixture over the leeks and cook in the air fryer for 10 minutes, or until the leeks are very tender. 4. Pat the fish dry and season with the remaining ½ teaspoon of salt and the pepper. When the leeks are ready, open the air fryer and place the fish fillets on top of the leeks. Air fry for 8 to 10 minutes, until the fish flakes easily with a fork (the thicker the fillets, the longer this will take). 5. While the fish cooks, make the coating: In a small bowl, combine the Parmesan, mayo, butter, and thyme. 6. When the fish is ready, remove it from the air fryer and increase the heat to 220ºC (or as high as your air fryer can go). Spread the fillets with a ½-inch-thick to ¾-inch-thick layer of the coating. 7. Place the fish back in the air fryer and air fry for 3 to 4 minutes, until the coating browns. 8. Garnish with fresh or dried thyme, if desired. Store leftovers in an airtight container in the refrigerator for up to 3 days. Reheat in a casserole dish in a preheated 180ºC air fryer for 6 minutes, or until heated through.

# Baked Tilapia with Garlic Aioli

**Prep time: 5 minutes | Cook time: 15 minutes | Serves 4**

Tilapia:
4 tilapia fillets
1 tablespoon extra-virgin olive oil
1 teaspoon garlic powder
1 teaspoon paprika
1 teaspoon dried basil
A pinch of lemon-pepper

seasoning
Garlic Aioli:
2 garlic cloves, minced
1 tablespoon mayonnaise
Juice of ½ lemon
1 teaspoon extra-virgin olive oil
Salt and pepper, to taste

1. Preheat the air fryer to 200ºC. 2. On a clean work surface, brush both sides of each fillet with the olive oil. Sprinkle with the garlic powder, paprika, basil, and lemon-pepper seasoning. 3. Place the fillets in the air fryer basket and bake for 15 minutes, flipping the fillets halfway through, or until the fish flakes easily and is no longer translucent in the center. 4. Meanwhile, make the garlic aioli: Whisk together the garlic, mayo, lemon juice, olive oil, salt, and pepper in a small bowl until smooth. 5. Remove the fish from the basket and serve with the garlic aioli on the side.

# Tandoori Prawns

**Prep time: 25 minutes | Cook time: 6 minutes | Serves 4**

455 g jumbo raw prawns (21 to 25 count), peeled and deveined
1 tablespoon minced fresh ginger
3 cloves garlic, minced
5 g chopped fresh coriander or parsley, plus more for garnish
1 teaspoon ground turmeric

1 teaspoon garam masala
1 teaspoon smoked paprika
1 teaspoon kosher or coarse sea salt
½ to 1 teaspoon cayenne pepper
2 tablespoons olive oil (for Paleo) or melted ghee
2 teaspoons fresh lemon juice

1. In a large bowl, combine the prawns, ginger, garlic, coriander, turmeric, garam masala, paprika, salt, and cayenne. Toss well to coat. Add the oil or ghee and toss again. Marinate at room temperature for 15 minutes, or cover and refrigerate for up to 8 hours. 2. Place the prawns in a single layer in the air fryer basket. Set the air fryer to 160ºC for 6 minutes. Transfer the prawns to a serving platter. Cover and let the prawns finish cooking in the residual heat, about 5 minutes. 3. Sprinkle the prawns with the lemon juice and toss to coat. Garnish with additional cilantro and serve.

# Easy Scallops

**Prep time: 5 minutes | Cook time: 4 minutes | Serves 2**

12 medium sea scallops, rinsed and patted dry
1 teaspoon fine sea salt
¾ teaspoon ground black

pepper, plus more for garnish
Fresh thyme leaves, for garnish (optional)
Avocado oil spray

1. Preheat the air fryer to 200ºC. Coat the air fryer basket with avocado oil spray. 2. Place the scallops in a medium bowl and spritz with avocado oil spray. Sprinkle the salt and pepper to season. 3. Transfer the seasoned scallops to the air fryer basket, spacing them apart. You may need to work in batches to avoid overcrowding. 4. Air fry for 4 minutes, flipping the scallops halfway through, or until the scallops are firm and reach an internal temperature of just 64ºC on a meat thermometer. 5. Remove from the basket and repeat with the remaining scallops. 6. Sprinkle the pepper and thyme leaves on top for garnish, if desired. Serve immediately.

# Nutty Prawns with Amaretto Glaze

**Prep time: 30 minutes | Cook time: 10 minutes per batch | Serves 10 to 12**

60 g plain flour
½ teaspoon baking powder
1 teaspoon salt
2 eggs, beaten
120 ml milk
2 tablespoons olive or vegetable

oil
185 g sliced almonds
900 g large prawns (about 32 to 40 prawns), peeled and deveined, tails left on
470 ml amaretto liqueur

1. Combine the flour, baking powder and salt in a large bowl. Add the eggs, milk and oil and stir until it forms a smooth batter. Coarsely crush the sliced almonds into a second shallow dish with your hands. 2. Dry the prawns well with paper towels. Dip the prawns into the batter and shake off any excess batter, leaving just enough to lightly coat the prawns. Transfer the prawns to the dish with the almonds and coat completely. Place the coated prawns on a plate or baking sheet and when all the prawns have been coated, freeze the prawns for an 1 hour, or as long as a week before air frying. 3. Preheat the air fryer to 200ºC. 4. Transfer 8 frozen prawns at a time to the air fryer basket. Air fry for 6 minutes. Turn the prawns over and air fry for an additional 4 minutes. Repeat with the remaining prawns. 5. While the prawns are cooking, bring the Amaretto to a boil in a small saucepan on the stovetop. Lower the heat and simmer until it has reduced and thickened into a glaze, about 10 minutes. 6. Remove the prawns from the air fryer and brush both sides with the warm amaretto glaze. Serve warm.

## chilli Lime Prawns

**Prep time: 5 minutes | Cook time: 5 minutes | Serves 4**

455 g medium prawns, peeled and deveined
1 tablespoon salted butter, melted
2 teaspoons chilli powder
¼ teaspoon garlic powder
¼ teaspoon salt
¼ teaspoon ground black pepper
½ small lime, zested and juiced, divided

1. In a medium bowl, toss prawns with butter, then sprinkle with chilli powder, garlic powder, salt, pepper, and lime zest. 2. Place prawns into ungreased air fryer basket. Adjust the temperature to 200ºC and air fry for 5 minutes. Prawns will be firm and form a "C" shape when done. 3. Transfer prawns to a large serving dish and drizzle with lime juice. Serve warm.

## Sweet Tilapia Fillets

**Prep time: 5 minutes | Cook time: 14 minutes | Serves 4**

2 tablespoons granulated sweetener
1 tablespoon apple cider
vinegar
4 tilapia fillets, boneless
1 teaspoon olive oil

1. Mix apple cider vinegar with olive oil and sweetener. 2. Then rub the tilapia fillets with the sweet mixture and put in the air fryer basket in one layer. Cook the fish at 180ºC for 7 minutes per side.

## Greek Fish Pitas

**Prep time: 10 minutes | Cook time: 15 minutes | Serves 4**

455 g pollock, cut into 1-inch pieces
60 ml olive oil
1 teaspoon salt
½ teaspoon dried oregano
½ teaspoon dried thyme
½ teaspoon garlic powder
¼ teaspoon cayenne
4 whole wheat pitas
75 g shredded lettuce
2 plum tomatoes, diced
Nonfat plain Greek yogurt
Lemon, quartered

1. Preheat the air fryer to 190ºC. 2. In a medium bowl, combine the pollock with olive oil, salt, oregano, thyme, garlic powder, and cayenne. 3. Put the pollock into the air fryer basket and roast for 15 minutes. 4. Serve inside pitas with lettuce, tomato, and Greek yogurt with a lemon wedge on the side.

## Browned Prawns Patties

**Prep time: 15 minutes | Cook time: 10 to 12 minutes | Serves 4**

230 g raw prawns, peeled, deveined and chopped finely
500 g cooked sushi rice
35 g chopped red bell pepper
35 g chopped celery
35 g chopped spring onion
2 teaspoons Worcestershire
sauce
½ teaspoon salt
½ teaspoon garlic powder
½ teaspoon Old Bay seasoning
75 g plain bread crumbs
Cooking spray

1. Preheat the air fryer to 200ºC. 2. Put all the ingredients except the bread crumbs and oil in a large bowl and stir to incorporate. 3. Scoop out the prawn mixture and shape into 8 equal-sized patties with your hands, no more than ½-inch thick. Roll the patties in the bread crumbs on a plate and spray both sides with cooking spray. 4. Place the patties in the air fryer basket. You may need to work in batches to avoid overcrowding. 5. Air fry for 10 to 12 minutes, flipping the patties halfway through, or until the outside is crispy brown. 6. Divide the patties among four plates and serve warm.

## Parmesan–Crusted Hake with Garlic Sauce

**Prep time: 5 minutes | Cook time: 10 minutes | Serves 3**

Fish:
6 tablespoons mayonnaise
1 tablespoon fresh lime juice
1 teaspoon Dijon mustard
150 g grated Parmesan cheese
Salt, to taste
¼ teaspoon ground black pepper, or more to taste
3 hake fillets, patted dry
Nonstick cooking spray
Garlic Sauce:
60 ml plain Greek yogurt
2 tablespoons olive oil
2 cloves garlic, minced
½ teaspoon minced tarragon leaves

1. Preheat the air fryer to 200ºC. 2. Mix the mayo, lime juice, and mustard in a shallow bowl and whisk to combine. In another shallow bowl, stir together the grated Parmesan cheese, salt, and pepper. 3. Dredge each fillet in the mayo mixture, then roll them in the cheese mixture until they are evenly coated on both sides. 4. Spray the air fryer basket with nonstick cooking spray. Arrange the fillets in the basket and air fry for 10 minutes, or until the fish flakes easily with a fork. Flip the fillets halfway through the cooking time. 5. Meanwhile, in a small bowl, whisk all the ingredients for the sauce until well incorporated. 6. Serve the fish warm alongside the sauce.

# Tuna Patty Sliders

**Prep time: 15 minutes | Cook time: 10 to 15 minutes | Serves 4**

3 cans tuna, 140 g each, packed in water
20 g whole-wheat panko bread crumbs
50 g shredded Parmesan cheese
1 tablespoon Sriracha
¾ teaspoon black pepper
10 whole-wheat buns
Cooking spray

1. Preheat the air fryer to 180ºC. 2. Spray the air fryer basket lightly with cooking spray. 3. In a medium bowl combine the tuna, bread crumbs, Parmesan cheese, Sriracha, and black pepper and stir to combine. 4. Form the mixture into 10 patties. 5. Place the patties in the air fryer basket in a single layer. Spray the patties lightly with cooking spray. You may need to cook them in batches. 6. Air fry for 6 to 8 minutes. Turn the patties over and lightly spray with cooking spray. Air fry until golden brown and crisp, another 4 to 7 more minutes. Serve warm.

# Tuna Melt

**Prep time: 3 minutes | Cook time: 10 minutes | Serves 1**

Olive or vegetable oil, for spraying
140 g canned tuna, drained
1 tablespoon mayonnaise
¼ teaspoon garlic granules, plus
more for garnish
2 teaspoons unsalted butte
2 slices sandwich bread of choice
2 slices Cheddar cheese

1. Line the air fryer basket with baking paper and spray lightly with oil. 2. In a medium bowl, mix together the tuna, mayonnaise, and garlic. 3. Spread 1 teaspoon of butter on each slice of bread and place one slice butter-side down in the prepared basket. 4. Top with a slice of cheese, the tuna mixture, another slice of cheese, and the other slice of bread, butter-side up. 5. Air fry at 200ºC for 5 minutes, flip, and cook for another 5 minutes, until browned and crispy. 6. Sprinkle with additional garlic, before cutting in half and serving.

# Prawns Scampi

**Prep time: 8 minutes | Cook time: 8 minutes | Serves 4**

4 tablespoons salted butter or ghee
1 tablespoon fresh lemon juice
1 tablespoon minced garlic
2 teaspoons red pepper flakes
455 g prawns (21 to 25 count), peeled and deveined
2 tablespoons dry white wine or chicken broth
2 tablespoons chopped fresh basil, plus more for sprinkling, or 1 tablespoon dried
1 tablespoon chopped fresh chives, or 1 teaspoon dried

1. Place a baking pan in the air fryer basket. Set the air fryer to 160ºC for 8 minutes (this will preheat the pan so the butter will melt faster). 2. Carefully remove the pan from the fryer and add the butter, lemon juice, garlic, and red pepper flakes. Place the pan back in the fryer. 3. Cook for 2 minutes, stirring once, until the butter has melted. (Do not skip this step; this is what infuses the butter with garlic flavour, which is what makes it all taste so good.) 4. Carefully remove the pan from the fryer and add the prawns, broth, basil, and chives. Stir gently until the ingredients are well combined. 5. Return the pan to the air fryer and cook for 5 minutes, stirring once. 6. Thoroughly stir the prawn mixture and let it rest for 1 minute on a wire rack. (This is so the prawns cook in the residual heat rather than getting overcooked and rubbery.) 7. Stir once more, sprinkle with additional chopped fresh basil, and serve.

# Cajun and Lemon Pepper Cod

**Prep time: 5 minutes | Cook time: 12 minutes | Makes 2 cod fillets**

1 tablespoon Cajun seasoning
1 teaspoon salt
½ teaspoon lemon pepper
½ teaspoon freshly ground black pepper
2 cod fillets, 230 g each, cut to
fit into the air fryer basket
Cooking spray
2 tablespoons unsalted butter, melted
1 lemon, cut into 4 wedges

1. Preheat the air fryer to 180ºC. Spritz the air fryer basket with cooking spray. 2. Thoroughly combine the Cajun seasoning, salt, lemon pepper, and black pepper in a small bowl. Rub this mixture all over the cod fillets until completely coated. 3. Put the fillets in the air fryer basket and brush the melted butter over both sides of each fillet. 4. Bake in the preheated air fryer for 12 minutes, flipping the fillets halfway through, or until the fish flakes easily with a fork. 5. Remove the fillets from the basket and serve with fresh lemon wedges.

# Chapter 7 Snacks and Appetizers

# Chapter 7 Snacks and Appetizers

## Crispy Filo Artichoke Triangles

**Prep time: 15 minutes | Cook time: 9 to 12 minutes |**
**Makes 18 triangles**

70 g Ricotta cheese
1 egg white
60 g minced and drained
artichoke hearts
3 tablespoons grated mozzarella

cheese cheese
½ teaspoon dried thyme
6 sheets frozen filo pastry,
thawed
2 tablespoons melted butter

1. Preheat the air fryer to 200ºC. 2. In a small bowl, combine the Ricotta cheese, egg white, artichoke hearts, mozzarella cheese cheese, and thyme, and mix well. 3. Cover the filo pastry with a damp kitchen towel while you work so it doesn't dry out. Using one sheet at a time, place on the work surface and cut into thirds lengthwise. 4. Put about 1½ teaspoons of the filling on each strip at the base. Fold the bottom right-hand tip of phyllo over the filling to meet the other side in a triangle, then continue folding in a triangle. Brush each triangle with butter to seal the edges. Repeat with the remaining phyllo dough and filling. 5. Place the triangles in the air fryer basket. Bake, 6 at a time, for about 3 to 4 minutes, or until the filo is golden and crisp. 6. Serve hot.

## Classic Spring Rolls

**Prep time: 10 minutes | Cook time: 9 minutes |**
**Makes 16 spring rolls**

4 teaspoons toasted sesame oil
6 medium garlic cloves, minced
or pressed
1 tablespoon grated peeled
fresh ginger
70 g thinly sliced shiitake
mushrooms
500 g chopped green cabbage

80 g grated carrot
½ teaspoon sea salt
16 rice paper wrappers
Cooking oil spray (sunflower,
safflower, or refined coconut)
Gluten-free sweet and sour
sauce or Thai sweet chilli sauce,
for serving (optional)

1. Place a wok or sauté pan over medium heat until hot. 2. Add the sesame oil, garlic, ginger, mushrooms, cabbage, carrot, and salt. Cook for 3 to 4 minutes, stirring often, until the cabbage is lightly wilted. Remove the pan from the heat. 3. Gently run a rice paper under water. Lay it on a flat non-absorbent surface. Place about 30 g of the cabbage filling in the middle. Once the wrapper is soft enough to roll, fold the bottom up over the filling, fold in the sides, and roll the wrapper all the way up. (Basically, make a tiny burrito.) 4. Repeat step 3 to make the remaining spring rolls until you have the number of spring rolls you want to cook right now (and the amount that will fit in the air fryer basket in a single layer without them touching each other). Refrigerate any leftover filling in an airtight container for about 1 week. 5. Insert the crisper plate into the basket and the basket into the unit. Preheat the unit by selecting AIR FRY, setting the temperature to 200ºC, and setting the time to 3 minutes. Select START/STOP to begin. 6. Once the unit is preheated, spray the crisper plate and the basket with cooking oil. Place the spring rolls into the basket, leaving a little room between them so they don't stick to each other. Spray the top of each spring roll with cooking oil. 7. Select AIR FRY, set the temperature to 200ºC, and set the time to 9 minutes. Select START/STOP to begin. 8. When the cooking is complete, the egg rolls should be crisp-ish and lightly browned. Serve immediately, plain or with a sauce of choice.

## Bacon–Wrapped A Pickled Gherkin Spear

**Prep time: 10 minutes | Cook time: 8 minutes |**
**Serves 4**

8 to 12 slices bacon
60 g soft white cheese
40 g shredded mozzarella
cheese cheese

8 fresh dill a pickled gherkin
spears
120 ml ranch dressing

1. Lay the bacon slices on a flat surface. In a medium-sized bowl, combine the soft white cheese and mozzarella cheese. stir until thoroughly combined. Spread the cheese mixture over the bacon slices. 2. Place a a pickled gherkin spear on a bacon slice and roll the bacon around the pickle in a spiral, ensuring the pickle is fully covered. (You may need to use more than one slice of bacon per pickle to fully cover the spear.) Fold in the ends to ensure the bacon stays put. Repeat to wrap all the pickled cucumbers. 3. Place the wrapped pickled cucumbers in the air fryer basket in a single layer. Set the air fryer to 200ºC for 8 minutes, or until the bacon is fully cooked and crisp on the edges. 4. Serve the a pickled gherkin spears with ranch dressing on the side.

# Jalapeño Poppers

**Prep time: 10 minutes | Cook time: 20 minutes |**
**Serves 4**

| | |
|---|---|
| Oil, for spraying | parsley |
| 227 g soft white cheese | ½ teaspoon granulated garlic |
| 177 ml gluten-free | ½ teaspoon salt |
| breadcrumbs, divided | 10 jalapeño peppers, halved and |
| 2 tablespoons chopped fresh | seeded |

1. Line the air fryer basket with parchment and spray lightly with oil. 2. In a medium bowl, mix together the soft white cheese, half of the breadcrumbs, the parsley, garlic, and salt. 3. Spoon the mixture into the jalapeño halves. Gently press the stuffed jalapeños in the remaining breadcrumbs. 4. Place the stuffed jalapeños in the prepared basket. 5. Air fry at 188°C for 20 minutes, or until the cheese is melted and the breadcrumbs are crisp and golden brown.

# Five–Ingredient Falafel with Garlic–Yoghurt Sauce

**Prep time: 5 minutes | Cook time: 15 minutes |**
**Serves 4**

| | |
|---|---|
| Falafel: | Garlic-Yoghurt Sauce: |
| 1 (425 g) can chickpeas, | 240 ml non-fat plain Greek |
| drained and rinsed | yoghurt |
| 30 g fresh parsley | 1 garlic clove, minced |
| 2 garlic cloves, minced | 1 tablespoon chopped fresh |
| ½ tablespoon cumin powder | fresh dill |
| 1 tablespoon wholemeal flour | 2 tablespoons lemon juice |
| Salt | |

Make the Falafel: 1. Preheat the air fryer to 180°C. 2. Put the chickpeas into a food processor. Pulse until mostly chopped, then add the parsley, garlic, and cumin and pulse for another 1 to 2 minutes, or until the ingredients are combined and turning into a dough. 3. Add the flour. Pulse a few more times until combined. The dough will have texture, but the chickpeas should be pulsed into small bits. 4. Using clean hands, roll the dough into 8 balls of equal size, then pat the balls down a bit so they are about ½-thick disks. 5. Spray the basket of the air fryer with olive oil cooking spray, then place the falafel burger patties in the basket in a single layer, making sure they don't touch each other. 6. Fry in the air fryer for 15 minutes. Make the garlic-yoghurt sauce 7. In a small bowl, combine the yoghurt, garlic, fresh dill, and lemon juice. 8. Once the falafel is done cooking and nicely browned on all sides, remove them from the air fryer and season with salt. 9. Serve hot with a side of dipping sauce.

# Crispy Green Bean Fries with Lemon–Yoghurt Sauce

**Prep time: 5 minutes | Cook time: 5 minutes | Serves 4**

| | |
|---|---|
| French beans: | 227 g whole French beans |
| 1 egg | Lemon-Yoghurt Sauce: |
| 2 tablespoons water | 120 ml non-fat plain Greek |
| 1 tablespoon wholemeal flour | yoghurt |
| ¼ teaspoon paprika | 1 tablespoon lemon juice |
| ½ teaspoon garlic powder | ¼ teaspoon salt |
| ½ teaspoon salt | ⅛ teaspoon cayenne pepper |
| 25 g wholemeal breadcrumbs | |

Make the French beans: 1. Preheat the air fryer to 190°C. 2. In a medium shallow dish, beat together the egg and water until frothy. 3. In a separate medium shallow dish, whisk together the flour, paprika, garlic powder, and salt, then mix in the breadcrumbs. 4. Spray the bottom of the air fryer with cooking spray. 5. Dip each green bean into the egg mixture, then into the bread crumb mixture, coating the outside with the crumbs. Place the French beans in a single layer in the bottom of the air fryer basket. 6. Fry in the air fryer for 5 minutes, or until the breading is golden. Make the Lemon-Yoghurt Sauce: 7. In a small bowl, combine the yoghurt, lemon juice, salt, and cayenne. 8. Serve the green bean fries alongside the lemon-yoghurt sauce as a snack or appetizer.

# Browned Ricotta with Capers and Lemon

**Prep time: 10 minutes | Cook time: 8 to 10 minutes |**
**Serves 4 to 6**

| | |
|---|---|
| 320 g whole milk ricotta cheese | rosemary |
| 2 tablespoons extra-virgin olive | Pinch crushed red pepper flakes |
| oil | Salt and freshly ground black |
| 2 tablespoons capers, rinsed | pepper, to taste |
| Zest of 1 lemon, plus more for | 1 tablespoon grated Parmesan |
| garnish | cheese |
| 1 teaspoon finely chopped fresh | |

1. Preheat the air fryer to 190°C. 2. In a mixing bowl, stir together the ricotta cheese, olive oil, capers, lemon zest, rosemary, red pepper flakes, salt, and pepper until well combined. 3. Spread the mixture evenly in a baking dish and place it in the air fryer basket. 4. Air fry for 8 to 10 minutes until the top is nicely browned. 5. Remove from the basket and top with a sprinkle of grated Parmesan cheese. 6. Garnish with the lemon zest and serve warm.

# String Bean Fries

**Prep time: 15 minutes | Cook time: 5 to 6 minutes | Serves 4**

227 g fresh French beans
2 eggs
4 teaspoons water
60 g plain flour
50 g breadcrumbs
¼ teaspoon salt

¼ teaspoon ground black pepper
¼ teaspoon mustard powder (optional)
Oil for misting or cooking spray

1. Preheat the air fryer to 180°C. 2. Trim stem ends from French beans, wash, and pat dry. 3. In a shallow dish, beat eggs and water together until well blended. 4. Place flour in a second shallow dish. 5. In a third shallow dish, stir together the breadcrumbs, salt, pepper, and mustard powder if using. 6. Dip each bean in egg mixture, flour, egg mixture again, then breadcrumbs. 7. When you finish coating all the French beans, open air fryer and place them in basket. 8. Cook for 3 minutes. 9. Stop and mist French beans with oil or cooking spray. 10. Cook for 2 to 3 more minutes or until French beans are crispy and nicely browned.

# Sweet Bacon Potato Crunchies

**Prep time: 5 minutes | Cook time: 7 minutes | Serves 4**

24 frozen potato crisps
6 slices cooked bacon

2 tablespoons maple syrup
110 g shredded Cheddar cheese

1. Preheat the air fryer to 200°C. 2. Put the potato crisps in the air fryer basket. Air fry for 10 minutes, shaking the basket halfway through the cooking time. 3. Meanwhile, cut the bacon into 1-inch pieces. 4. Remove the potato crisps from the air fryer basket and put into a baking pan. Top with the bacon and drizzle with the maple syrup. Air fry for 5 minutes, or until the crunchies and bacon are crisp. 5. Top with the cheese and air fry for 2 minutes, or until the cheese is melted. 6. Serve hot.

# Old Bay Chicken Wings

**Prep time: 10 minutes | Cook time: 12 to 15 minutes | Serves 4**

2 tablespoons Old Bay or all-purpose seasoning
2 teaspoons baking powder

2 teaspoons salt
900 g chicken wings, patted dry
Cooking spray

1. Preheat the air fryer to 200°C. Lightly spray the air fryer basket with cooking spray. 2. Combine the seasoning, baking powder, and salt in a large zip-top plastic bag. Add the chicken wings, seal, and shake until the wings are thoroughly coated in the seasoning mixture. 3. Lay the chicken wings in the air fryer basket in a single layer and lightly mist with cooking spray. You may need to work in batches to avoid overcrowding. 4. Air fry for 12 to 15 minutes, flipping the wings halfway through, or until the wings are lightly browned and the internal temperature reaches at least 74°C on a meat thermometer. 5. Remove from the basket to a plate and repeat with the remaining chicken wings. 6. Serve hot.

# Air Fried Pot Stickers

**Prep time: 10 minutes | Cook time: 18 to 20 minutes | Makes 30 pot stickers**

35 g finely chopped cabbage
30 g finely chopped red pepper
2 spring onions, finely chopped
1 egg, beaten
2 tablespoons cocktail sauce

2 teaspoons low-salt soy sauce
30 wonton wrappers
1 tablespoon water, for brushing the wrappers

1. Preheat the air fryer to 180°C. 2. In a small bowl, combine the cabbage, pepper, spring onions, egg, cocktail sauce, and soy sauce, and mix well. 3. Put about 1 teaspoon of the mixture in the centre of each wonton wrapper. Fold the wrapper in half, covering the filling; dampen the edges with water, and seal. You can crimp the edges of the wrapper with your fingers, so they look like the pot stickers you get in restaurants. Brush them with water. 4. Place the pot stickers in the air fryer basket and air fry in 2 batches for 9 to 10 minutes, or until the pot stickers are hot and the bottoms are lightly browned. 5. Serve hot.

# Ranch Oyster Snack Crackers

**Prep time: 3 minutes | Cook time: 12 minutes | Serves 6**

Oil, for spraying
60 ml olive oil
2 teaspoons dry ranch dressing mix
1 teaspoon chili powder
½ teaspoon dried fresh dill

weed
½ teaspoon garlic powder
½ teaspoon salt
1 (255 g) bag water biscuits or low-salt biscuits

1. Preheat the air fryer to 160°C. Line the air fryer basket with baking paper and spray lightly with oil. 2. In a large bowl, mix together the olive oil, ranch dressing mix, chili powder, fresh dill, garlic, and salt. Add the crackers and toss until evenly coated. 3. Place the mixture in the prepared basket. 4. Cook for 10 to 12 minutes, shaking or stirring every 3 to 4 minutes, or until crisp and golden.

## Tangy Fried A Pickle Gherkin Spears

**Prep time: 5 minutes | Cook time: 15 minutes | Serves 6**

| | |
|---|---|
| 2 jars sweet and sour a pickled gherkin spears, patted dry | 1 teaspoon sea salt |
| 2 medium-sized eggs | ½ teaspoon shallot powder |
| 80 ml milk | ⅓ teaspoon chili powder |
| 1 teaspoon garlic powder | 80 g plain flour |
| | Cooking spray |

1. Preheat the air fryer to 200°C. Spritz the air fryer basket with cooking spray. 2. In a bowl, beat together the eggs with milk. In another bowl, combine garlic powder, sea salt, shallot powder, chili powder and plain flour until well blended. 3. One by one, roll the a pickled gherkin spears in the powder mixture, then dredge them in the egg mixture. Dip them in the powder mixture a second time for additional coating. 4. Arrange the coated pickled cucumbers in the prepared basket. Air fry for 15 minutes until golden and crispy, shaking the basket halfway through to ensure even cooking. 5. Transfer to a plate and let cool for 5 minutes before serving.

## Crispy Mozzarella Cheese Sticks

**Prep time: 8 minutes | Cook time: 5 minutes | Serves 4**

| | |
|---|---|
| 65 g plain flour | ½ teaspoon garlic salt |
| 1 egg, beaten | 6 mozzarella cheese sticks, |
| 25 g panko breadcrumbs | halved crosswise |
| 30 g grated Parmesan cheese | Olive oil spray |
| 1 teaspoon Italian seasoning | |

1. Put the flour in a small bowl. 2. Put the beaten egg in another small bowl. 3. In a medium-sized bowl, stir together the panko, Parmesan cheese, Italian seasoning, and garlic salt. 4. Roll a mozzarella cheese-stick half in the flour, dip it into the egg, and then roll it in the panko mixture to coat. Press the coating lightly to make sure the breadcrumbs stick to the cheese. Repeat with the remaining 11 mozzarella cheese sticks. 5. Insert the crisper plate into the basket and the basket into the unit. Preheat the unit by selecting AIR FRY, setting the temperature to 200°C, and setting the time to 3 minutes. Select START/STOP to begin. 6. Once the unit is preheated, spray the crisper plate with olive oil and place a baking paper paper liner in the basket. Place the mozzarella cheese sticks into the basket and lightly spray them with olive oil. 7. Select AIR FRY, set the temperature to 200°C, and set the time to 5 minutes. Select START/STOP to begin. 8. When the cooking is complete, the mozzarella cheese sticks should be golden and crispy. Let the sticks stand for 1 minute before transferring them to a serving plate. Serve warm.

## Mixed Vegetables Pot Stickers

**Prep time: 12 minutes | Cook time: 11 to 18 minutes | Makes 12 pot stickers**

| | |
|---|---|
| 70 g shredded red cabbage | 2 garlic cloves, minced |
| 25 g chopped button mushrooms | 2 teaspoons grated fresh ginger |
| 35 g grated carrot | 12 gyoza/pot sticker wrappers |
| 2 tablespoons minced onion | 2½ teaspoons olive oil, divided |

1. In a baking pan, combine the red cabbage, mushrooms, carrot, onion, garlic, and ginger. Add 1 tablespoon of water. Place in the air fryer and air fry at 190°C for 3 to 6 minutes, until the mixed vegetables are crisp-tender. Drain and set aside. 2. Working one at a time, place the pot sticker wrappers on a work surface. Top each wrapper with a scant 1 tablespoon of the filling. Fold half of the wrapper over the other half to form a half circle. Dab one edge with water and press both edges together. 3. To another pan, add 1¼ teaspoons of olive oil. Put half of the pot stickers, seam-side up, in the pan. Air fry for 5 minutes, or until the bottoms are light golden. Add 1 tablespoon of water and return the pan to the air fryer. 4. Air fry for 4 to 6 minutes more, or until hot. Repeat with the remaining pot stickers, remaining 1¼ teaspoons of oil, and another tablespoon of water. Serve immediately.

## Lemon Prawns with Garlic Olive Oil

**Prep time: 5 minutes | Cook time: 6 minutes | Serves 4**

| | |
|---|---|
| 340 g medium prawns, cleaned and deveined | ½ teaspoon salt |
| 60 ml plus 2 tablespoons olive oil, divided | ¼ teaspoon red pepper flakes |
| Juice of ½ lemon | Lemon wedges, for serving (optional) |
| 3 garlic cloves, minced and divided | Marinara sauce, for dipping (optional) |

1. Preheat the air fryer to 190°C. 2. In a large bowl, combine the prawns with 2 tablespoons of the olive oil, as well as the lemon juice, ⅓ of the minced garlic, salt, and red pepper flakes. Toss to coat the prawns well. 3. In a small ramekin, combine the remaining 60 ml of olive oil and the remaining minced garlic. 4. Tear off a 12-by-12-inch sheet of aluminium foil. Pour the prawns into the centre of the foil, then fold the sides up and crimp the edges so that it forms an aluminium foil bowl that is open on top. Place this packet into the air fryer basket. 5. Roast the prawns for 4 minutes, then open the air fryer and place the ramekin with oil and garlic in the basket beside the prawns packet. Cook for 2 more minutes. 6. Transfer the prawns on a serving plate or platter with the ramekin of garlic olive oil on the side for dipping. You may also serve with lemon wedges and marinara sauce, if desired.

# Cheese Drops

**Prep time: 15 minutes | Cook time: 10 minutes per batch | Serves 8**

| | |
|---|---|
| 90 g plain flour | (optional) |
| ½ teaspoon rock salt | 57 g butter, softened |
| ¼ teaspoon cayenne pepper | 100 g grated extra mature |
| ¼ teaspoon smoked paprika | cheddar cheese, at room |
| ¼ teaspoon black pepper | temperature |
| a dash of garlic powder | Olive oil spray |

1. 1.In a small bowl, combine the flour, salt, cayenne, paprika, pepper, and garlic powder, if using. 2. Using a food processor, cream the butter and cheese until smooth. Gently add the seasoned flour and process until the dough is well combined, smooth, and no longer sticky. (Or make the dough in a stand mixer fitted with the paddle attachment: Cream the butter and cheese at medium speed until smooth, then add the seasoned flour and beat at low speed until smooth.) 3. Divide the dough into 32 pieces of equal size. On a lightly floured surface, roll each piece into a small ball. 4. Spray the air fryer basket with oil spray. Arrange 16 cheese drops in the basket. Set the air fryer to 160°C for 10 minutes, or until drops are just starting to brown. Transfer to a a wire rack. Repeat with remaining dough, checking for degree of doneness at 8 minutes. 5. Cool the cheese drops completely on the a wire rack. Store in an airtight container until ready to serve, or up to 1 or 2 days.

# Hush Puppies

**Prep time: 45 minutes | Cook time: 10 minutes | Serves 12**

| | |
|---|---|
| 144 g self-raising yellow cornmeal | 1 large egg |
| | 80 g canned creamed sweetcorn |
| 60 g plain flour | 216 g minced onion |
| 1 teaspoon sugar | 2 teaspoons minced jalapeño |
| 1 teaspoon salt | chillies pepper |
| 1 teaspoon freshly ground black pepper | 2 tablespoons olive oil, divided |

1. Thoroughly combine the cornmeal, flour, sugar, salt, and pepper in a large bowl. 2. Whisk together the egg and sweetcorn in a small bowl. Pour the egg mixture into the bowl of cornmeal mixture and stir to combine. Stir in the minced onion and jalapeño chillies. Cover the bowl with plastic wrap and place in the refrigerator for 30 minutes. 3. Preheat the air fryer to 190°C. Line the air fryer basket with baking paper paper and lightly brush it with 1 tablespoon of olive oil. 4. Scoop out the cornmeal mixture and form into 24 balls, about 1 inch. 5. Arrange the balls in the baking paper paper-lined basket, leaving space between each ball. 6. Air fry in batches for 5 minutes. Shake the basket and brush the balls with the remaining 1 tablespoon of olive oil. Continue cooking for 5 minutes until golden. 7. Remove the balls (hush puppies) from the basket and serve on a plate.

# Kale Chips with Tex–Mex Dip

**Prep time: 10 minutes | Cook time: 5 to 6 minutes | Serves 8**

| | |
|---|---|
| 240 ml Greek yoghurt | 1 bunch curly kale |
| 1 tablespoon chili powder | 1 teaspoon olive oil |
| 80 ml low-salt salsa, well drained | ¼ teaspoon coarse sea salt |

1. In a small bowl, combine the yoghurt, chili powder, and drained salsa; refrigerate. 2. Rinse the kale thoroughly, and pat dry. Remove the stems and ribs from the kale, using a sharp knife. Cut or tear the leaves into 3-inch pieces. 3. Toss the kale with the olive oil in a large bowl. 4. Air fry the kale in small batches at 200°C until the leaves are crisp. This should take 5 to 6 minutes. Shake the basket once during cooking time. 5. As you remove the kale chips, sprinkle them with a bit of the sea salt. 6. When all of the kale chips are done, serve with the dip.

# Pepperoni Pizza Dip

**Prep time: 10 minutes | Cook time: 10 minutes | Serves 6**

| | |
|---|---|
| 170 g soft white cheese | 42 g sliced miniature pepperoni |
| 85 g shredded Italian cheese blend | 400 g sliced black olives |
| | 1 tablespoon thinly sliced |
| 60 ml soured cream | spring onion |
| 1½ teaspoons dried Italian seasoning | Cut-up raw mixed vegetables, toasted baguette slices, pitta |
| ¼ teaspoon garlic salt | chips, or tortilla chips, for |
| ¼ teaspoon onion powder | serving |
| 165 g pizza sauce | |

1. In a small bowl, combine the soft white cheese, 28 g of the shredded cheese, the soured cream, Italian seasoning, garlic salt, and onion powder. Stir until smooth and the ingredients are well blended. 2. Spread the mixture in a baking pan. Top with the pizza sauce, spreading to the edges. Sprinkle with the remaining 56 g shredded cheese. Arrange the pepperoni slices on top of the cheese. Top with the black olives and green onion. 3. Place the pan in the air fryer basket. Set the air fryer to 180°C for 10 minutes, or until the pepperoni is beginning to brown on the edges and the cheese is bubbly and lightly browned. 4. Let stand for 5 minutes before serving with mixed vegetables, toasted baguette slices, pitta chips, or tortilla chips.

# Garlic–Roasted Tomatoes and Olives

**Prep time: 5 minutes | Cook time: 20 minutes |**

**Serves 6**

| | |
|---|---|
| 300 g cherry tomatoes | 1 tablespoon fresh basil, minced |
| 4 garlic cloves, roughly chopped | 1 tablespoon fresh oregano, minced |
| ½ red onion, roughly chopped | 2 tablespoons olive oil |
| 160 g black olives | ¼ to ½ teaspoon salt |
| 180 g green olives | |

1. Preheat the air fryer to 190ºC. 2. In a large bowl, combine all of the ingredients and toss together so that the tomatoes and olives are coated well with the olive oil and herbs. 3. Pour the mixture into the air fryer basket, and roast for 10 minutes. Stir the mixture well, then continue roasting for an additional 10 minutes. 4. Remove from the air fryer, transfer to a serving bowl, and enjoy.

# Bruschetta with Basil Pesto

**Prep time: 10 minutes | Cook time: 5 to 11 minutes |**

**Serves 4**

| | |
|---|---|
| 8 slices French bread, ½ inch thick | cheese cheese |
| 2 tablespoons softened butter | 120 g basil pesto |
| 120 g shredded mozzarella | 240 g chopped cherry tomatoes |
| | 2 spring onions, thinly sliced |

1. Preheat the air fryer to 180ºC. 2. Spread the bread with the butter and place butter-side up in the air fryer basket. Bake for 3 to 5 minutes, or until the bread is light golden. 3. Remove the bread from the basket and top each piece with some of the cheese. Return to the basket in 2 batches and bake for 1 to 3 minutes, or until the cheese melts. 4. Meanwhile, combine the pesto, tomatoes, and spring onions in a small bowl. 5. When the cheese has melted, remove the bread from the air fryer and place on a serving plate. Top each slice with some of the pesto mixture and serve.

# Pickle Chips

**Prep time: 30 minutes | Cook time: 12 minutes |**

**Serves 4**

| | |
|---|---|
| Oil, for spraying | 245 g plain flour |
| 40 g sliced fresh dill or 240 g sweet gherkins, drained | 2 large eggs, beaten |
| 240 ml buttermilk | 110 g panko breadcrumbs |
| | ¼ teaspoon salt |

1. Line the air fryer basket with baking paper and spray lightly with oil. 2. In a shallow dish, combine the pickled cucumbers and buttermilk and let soak for at least 1 hour, then drain. 3. Place the flour, beaten eggs, and breadcrumbs in separate bowls. 4. Coat each pickle chip lightly in the flour, dip in the eggs, and dredge in the breadcrumbs. Be sure each one is evenly coated. 5. Place the pickle chips in the prepared basket, sprinkle with the salt, and spray lightly with oil. You may need to work in batches, depending on the size of your air fryer. 6. Air fry at 200ºC for 5 minutes, flip, and cook for another 5 to 7 minutes, or until crispy. Serve hot.

# Stuffed Figs with Goat Cheese and Honey

**Prep time: 5 minutes | Cook time: 10 minutes |**

**Serves 4**

| | |
|---|---|
| 8 fresh figs | 1 tablespoon honey, plus more for serving |
| 57 g goat cheese | |
| ¼ teaspoon cinnamon powder | 1 tablespoon olive oil |

1. Preheat the air fryer to 180ºC. Line an 8-by-8-inch baking dish with baking paper paper that comes up the side so you can lift it out after cooking. 2. In a large bowl, mix together all of the ingredients until well combined. 3. Press the oat mixture into the pan in an even layer. 4. Place the pan into the air fryer basket and bake for 15 minutes. 5. Remove the pan from the air fryer and lift the granola cake out of the pan using the edges of the baking paper paper. 6. Allow to cool for 5 minutes before slicing into 6 equal bars. 7. Serve immediately or wrap in plastic wrap and store at room temperature for up to 1 week.

# Artichoke and Olive Pitta Flatbread

**Prep time: 5 minutes | Cook time: 10 minutes |**

**Serves 4**

| | |
|---|---|
| 2 wholewheat pitta bread | 70 g Kalamata olives |
| 2 tablespoons olive oil, divided | 30 g shredded Parmesan |
| 2 garlic cloves, minced | 55 g crumbled feta cheese |
| ¼ teaspoon salt | Chopped fresh parsley, for garnish (optional) |
| 120 g canned artichoke hearts, sliced | |

1. Preheat the air fryer to 190ºC. 2. Brush each pitta with 1 tablespoon olive oil, then sprinkle the minced garlic and salt over the top. 3. Distribute the artichoke hearts, olives, and cheeses evenly between the two pitta bread, and place both into the air fryer to bake for 10 minutes. 4. Remove the pitta bread and cut them into 4 pieces each before serving. Sprinkle parsley over the top, if desired.

# Chapter 8 Vegetables and Sides

# Chapter 8 Vegetables and Sides

## Crispy Chickpeas

**Prep time: 5 minutes | Cook time: 15 minutes |**
**Serves 4**

1 (425 g) can chickpeas, drained but not rinsed
2 tablespoons olive oil

1 teaspoon salt
2 tablespoons lemon juice

1. Preheat the air fryer to 200ºC. 2. Add all the ingredients together in a bowl and mix. Transfer this mixture to the air fryer basket. 3. Air fry for 15 minutes, ensuring the chickpeas become nice and crispy. 4. Serve immediately.

## Caesar Whole Cauliflower

**Prep time: 20 minutes | Cook time: 30 minutes |**
**Serves 2 to 4**

3 tablespoons olive oil
2 tablespoons red wine vinegar
2 tablespoons Worcestershire sauce
2 tablespoons grated Parmesan cheese
1 tablespoon Dijon mustard
4 garlic cloves, minced
4 oil-packed anchovy fillets,

drained and finely minced
coarse sea salt and freshly ground black pepper, to taste
1 small head cauliflower (about 450 g), green leaves trimmed and stem trimmed flush with the bottom of the head
1 tablespoon roughly chopped fresh flat-leaf parsley (optional)

1. In a liquid measuring jug, whisk together the olive oil, vinegar, Worcestershire, Parmesan, mustard, garlic, anchovies, and salt and pepper to taste. Place the cauliflower head upside down on a cutting board and use a paring knife to make an "x" through the full length of the core. Transfer the cauliflower head to a large bowl and pour half the dressing over it. Turn the cauliflower head to coat it in the dressing, then let it rest, stem-side up, in the dressing for at least 10 minutes and up to 30 minutes to allow the dressing to seep into all its nooks and crannies. 2. Transfer the cauliflower head, stem-side down, to the air fryer and air fry at 170ºC or 25 minutes. Drizzle the remaining dressing over the cauliflower and air fry at 200ºC until the top of the cauliflower is golden brown and the core is tender, about 5 minutes more. 3. Remove the basket from the air fryer and transfer the cauliflower to a large plate. Sprinkle with the parsley, if you like, and serve hot.

## Sesame Carrots and Sugar Snap Peas

**Prep time: 10 minutes | Cook time: 16 minutes |**
**Serves 4**

450 g carrots, peeled sliced on the bias (½-inch slices)
1 teaspoon olive oil
Salt and freshly ground black pepper, to taste
110 g honey

1 tablespoon sesame oil
1 tablespoon soy sauce
½ teaspoon minced fresh ginger
110 g sugar snap peas
1½ teaspoons sesame seeds

1. Preheat the air fryer to 180ºC. 2. Toss the carrots with the olive oil, season with salt and pepper and air fry for 10 minutes, shaking the basket once or twice during the cooking process. 3. Combine the honey, sesame oil, soy sauce and minced ginger in a large bowl. Add the sugar snap peas and the air-fried carrots to the honey mixture, toss to coat and return everything to the air fryer basket. 4. Turn up the temperature to 200ºC and air fry for an additional 6 minutes, shaking the basket once during the cooking process. 5. Transfer the carrots and sugar snap peas to a serving bowl. Pour the sauce from the bottom of the cooker over the vegetables and sprinkle sesame seeds over top. Serve immediately.

## Rosemary–Roasted Red Potatoes

**Prep time: 5 minutes | Cook time: 20 minutes |**
**Serves 6**

450 g red potatoes, quartered
65 ml olive oil
½ teaspoon coarse sea salt

¼ teaspoon black pepper
1 garlic clove, minced
4 rosemary sprigs

1. Preheat the air fryer to 180ºC. 2. In a large bowl, toss the potatoes with the olive oil, salt, pepper, and garlic until well coated. 3. Pour the potatoes into the air fryer basket and top with the sprigs of rosemary. 4. Roast for 10 minutes, then stir or toss the potatoes and roast for 10 minutes more. 5. Remove the rosemary sprigs and serve the potatoes. Season with additional salt and pepper, if needed.

# Garlic–Parmesan Crispy Baby Potatoes

**Prep time: 10 minutes | Cook time: 15 minutes | Serves 4**

Oil, for spraying
450 g baby potatoes
45 g grated Parmesan cheese, divided
3 tablespoons olive oil
2 teaspoons garlic powder
½ teaspoon onion powder
½ teaspoon salt
¼ teaspoon freshly ground black pepper
¼ teaspoon paprika
2 tablespoons chopped fresh parsley, for garnish

1. Line the air fryer basket with parchment and spray lightly with oil. 2. Rinse the potatoes, pat dry with paper towels, and place in a large bowl. 3. In a small bowl, mix together 45 g of Parmesan cheese, the olive oil, garlic, onion powder, salt, black pepper, and paprika. Pour the mixture over the potatoes and toss to coat. 4. Transfer the potatoes to the prepared basket and spread them out in an even layer, taking care to keep them from touching. You may need to work in batches, depending on the size of your air fryer. 5. Air fry at 200ºC for 15 minutes, stirring after 7 to 8 minutes, or until easily pierced with a fork. Continue to cook for another 1 to 2 minutes, if needed. 6. Sprinkle with the parsley and the remaining Parmesan cheese and serve.

# Stuffed Red Peppers with Herbed Ricotta and Tomatoes

**Prep time: 10 minutes | Cook time: 20 minutes | Serves 4**

2 red peppers
250 g cooked brown rice
2 plum tomatoes, diced
1 garlic clove, minced
¼ teaspoon salt
¼ teaspoon black pepper
115 g ricotta
3 tablespoons fresh basil, chopped
3 tablespoons fresh oregano, chopped
20 g shredded Parmesan, for topping

1. Preheat the air fryer to 180ºC. 2. Cut the bell peppers in half and remove the seeds and stem. 3. In a medium bowl, combine the brown rice, tomatoes, garlic, salt, and pepper. 4. Distribute the rice filling evenly among the four bell pepper halves. 5. In a small bowl, combine the ricotta, basil, and oregano. Put the herbed cheese over the top of the rice mixture in each bell pepper. 6. Place the bell peppers into the air fryer and roast for 20 minutes. 7. Remove and serve with shredded Parmesan on top.

# Breaded Green Tomatoes

**Prep time: 15 minutes | Cook time: 30 minutes | Serves 4**

60 g plain flour
2 eggs
60 g semolina
60 g panko bread crumbs
1 teaspoon garlic powder
Salt and freshly ground black pepper, to taste
2 green tomatoes, cut into ½-inch-thick rounds
Cooking oil spray

1. Place the flour in a small bowl. 2. In another small bowl, beat the eggs. 3. In a third small bowl, stir together the semolina, panko, and garlic powder. Season with salt and pepper. 4. Dip each tomato slice into the flour, the egg, and finally the semolina mixture to coat. 5. Insert the crisper plate into the basket and the basket into the unit. Preheat the unit by selecting AIR FRY, setting the temperature to 200ºC, and setting the time to 3 minutes. Select START/STOP to begin. 6. Once the unit is preheated, spray the crisper plate and the basket with cooking oil. Working in batches, place the tomato slices in the air fryer in a single layer. Do not stack them. Spray the tomato slices with the cooking oil. 7. Select AIR FRY, set the temperature to 200ºC, and set the time to 10 minutes. Select START/STOP to begin. 8. After 5 minutes, use tongs to flip the tomatoes. Resume cooking for 4 to 5 minutes, or until crisp. 9. When the cooking is complete, transfer the fried green tomatoes to a plate. Repeat steps 6, 7, and 8 for the remaining tomatoes.

# Sausage–Stuffed Mushroom Caps

**Prep time: 10 minutes | Cook time: 8 minutes | Serves 2**

6 large portobello mushroom caps
230 g Italian sausage
15 g chopped onion
2 tablespoons blanched finely ground almond flour
20 g grated Parmesan cheese
1 teaspoon minced fresh garlic

1. Use a spoon to hollow out each mushroom cap, reserving scrapings. 2. In a medium skillet over medium heat, brown the sausage about 10 minutes or until fully cooked and no pink remains. Drain and then add reserved mushroom scrapings, onion, almond flour, Parmesan, and garlic. Gently fold ingredients together and continue cooking an additional minute, then remove from heat. 3. Evenly spoon the mixture into mushroom caps and place the caps into a 6-inch round pan. Place pan into the air fryer basket. 4. Adjust the temperature to 190ºC and set the timer for 8 minutes. 5. When finished cooking, the tops will be browned and bubbling. Serve warm.

## Zesty Fried Asparagus

**Prep time: 3 minutes | Cook time: 10 minutes |**
**Serves 4**

| | |
|---|---|
| Oil, for spraying | 1 tablespoon garlic powder |
| 10 to 12 spears asparagus, trimmed | 1 teaspoon chili powder |
| | ½ teaspoon ground cumin |
| 2 tablespoons olive oil | ¼ teaspoon salt |

1. Line the air fryer basket with parchment and spray lightly with oil. 2. If the asparagus are too long to fit easily in the air fryer, cut them in half. 3. Place the asparagus, olive oil, garlic, chili powder, cumin, and salt in a zip-top plastic bag, seal, and toss until evenly coated. 4. Place the asparagus in the prepared basket. 5. Roast at 200ºC for 5 minutes, flip, and cook for another 5 minutes, or until bright green and firm but tender.

## Garlic and Thyme Tomatoes

**Prep time: 10 minutes | Cook time: 15 minutes |**
**Serves 2 to 4**

| | |
|---|---|
| 4 plum tomatoes | pepper, to taste |
| 1 tablespoon olive oil | 1 clove garlic, minced |
| Salt and freshly ground black | ½ teaspoon dried thyme |

1. Preheat the air fryer to 200ºC. 2. Cut the tomatoes in half and scoop out the seeds and any pithy parts with your fingers. Place the tomatoes in a bowl and toss with the olive oil, salt, pepper, garlic and thyme. 3. Transfer the tomatoes to the air fryer, cut side up. Air fry for 15 minutes. The edges should just start to brown. Let the tomatoes cool to an edible temperature for a few minutes and then use in pastas, on top of crostini, or as an accompaniment to any poultry, meat or fish.

## Cauliflower Rice Balls

**Prep time: 10 minutes | Cook time: 8 minutes |**
**Serves 4**

| | |
|---|---|
| 1 (280 g) steamer bag cauliflower rice, cooked according to package instructions | 1 large egg |
| | 60 g plain pork scratchings, finely crushed |
| 110 g shredded Mozzarella cheese | ¼ teaspoon salt |
| | ½ teaspoon Italian seasoning |

1. Place cauliflower into a large bowl and mix with Mozzarella. 2. Whisk egg in a separate medium bowl. Place pork scratchings into another large bowl with salt and Italian seasoning. 3. Separate cauliflower mixture into four equal sections and form each into a ball. Carefully dip a ball into whisked egg, then roll in pork scratchings. Repeat with remaining balls. 4. Place cauliflower balls into ungreased air fryer basket. Adjust the temperature to 200ºC and air fry for 8 minutes. Rice balls will be golden when done. 5. Use a spatula to carefully move cauliflower balls to a large dish for serving. Serve warm.

## Roasted Radishes with Sea Salt

**Prep time: 5 minutes | Cook time: 18 minutes |**
**Serves 4**

| | |
|---|---|
| 450 g radishes, ends trimmed if needed | 2 tablespoons olive oil |
| | ½ teaspoon sea salt |

1. Preheat the air fryer to 180ºC. 2. In a large bowl, combine the radishes with olive oil and sea salt. 3. Pour the radishes into the air fryer and roast for 10 minutes. Stir or turn the radishes over and roast for 8 minutes more, then serve.

## Parmesan Herb Focaccia Bread

**Prep time: 10 minutes | Cook time: 10 minutes |**
**Serves 6**

| | |
|---|---|
| 225 g shredded Mozzarella cheese | ½ teaspoon bicarbonate of soda |
| | 2 large eggs |
| 30 g) full-fat cream cheese | ½ teaspoon garlic powder |
| 95 g blanched finely ground almond flour | ¼ teaspoon dried basil |
| | ¼ teaspoon dried rosemary |
| 40 g ground golden flaxseed | 2 tablespoons salted butter, melted and divided |
| 20 g grated Parmesan cheese | |

1. Place Mozzarella, cream cheese, and almond flour into a large microwave-safe bowl and microwave for 1 minute. Add the flaxseed, Parmesan, and bicarbonate of soda and stir until smooth ball forms. If the mixture cools too much, it will be hard to mix. Return to microwave for 10 to 15 seconds to rewarm if necessary. 2. Stir in eggs. You may need to use your hands to get them fully incorporated. Just keep stirring and they will absorb into the dough. 3. Sprinkle dough with garlic powder, basil, and rosemary and knead into dough. Grease a baking pan with 1 tablespoon melted butter. Press the dough evenly into the pan. Place pan into the air fryer basket. 4. Adjust the temperature to 200ºC and bake for 10 minutes. 5. At 7 minutes, cover with foil if bread begins to get too dark. 6. Remove and let cool at least 30 minutes. Drizzle with remaining butter and serve.

# Garlic Herb Radishes

**Prep time: 10 minutes | Cook time: 10 minutes |**

**Serves 4**

| | |
|---|---|
| 450 g radishes | ½ teaspoon dried parsley |
| 2 tablespoons unsalted butter, melted | ¼ teaspoon dried oregano |
| ½ teaspoon garlic powder | ¼ teaspoon ground black pepper |

1. Remove roots from radishes and cut into quarters. 2. In a small bowl, add butter and seasonings. Toss the radishes in the herb butter and place into the air fryer basket. 3. Adjust the temperature to 180°C and set the timer for 10 minutes. 4. Halfway through the cooking time, toss the radishes in the air fryer basket. Continue cooking until edges begin to turn brown. 5. Serve warm.

# Parmesan–Rosemary Radishes

**Prep time: 5 minutes | Cook time: 15 to 20 minutes |**

**Serves 4**

| | |
|---|---|
| 1 bunch radishes, stemmed, trimmed, and quartered | 1 tablespoon chopped fresh rosemary |
| 1 tablespoon avocado oil | Sea salt and freshly ground black pepper, to taste |
| 2 tablespoons finely grated fresh Parmesan cheese | |

1. Place the radishes in a medium bowl and toss them with the avocado oil, Parmesan cheese, rosemary, salt, and pepper. 2. Set the air fryer to190°C. Arrange the radishes in a single layer in the air fryer basket. Roast for 15 to 20 minutes, until golden brown and tender. Let cool for 5 minutes before serving.

# Caramelized Aubergine with Harissa Yogurt

**Prep time: 10 minutes | Cook time: 15 minutes |**

**Serves 2**

| | |
|---|---|
| 1 medium aubergine (about 340 g), cut crosswise into ½-inch-thick slices and quartered | ground black pepper, to taste |
| 2 tablespoons vegetable oil | 120 g plain yogurt (not Greek) |
| coarse sea salt and freshly | 2 tablespoons harissa paste |
| | 1 garlic clove, grated |
| | 2 teaspoons honey |

1. In a bowl, toss together the aubergine and oil, season with salt and pepper, and toss to coat evenly. Transfer to the air fryer and air fry at 200°C, shaking the basket every 5 minutes, until the aubergine is caramelized and tender, about 15 minutes. 2.

Meanwhile, in a small bowl, whisk together the yogurt, harissa, and garlic, then spread onto a serving plate. 3. Pile the warm aubergine over the yogurt and drizzle with the honey just before serving.

# Hawaiian Brown Rice

**Prep time: 10 minutes | Cook time: 12 to 16 minutes |**

**| Serves 4 to 6**

| | |
|---|---|
| 110 g ground sausage | 380 g cooked brown rice |
| 1 teaspoon butter | 1 (230 g) can crushed |
| 20 g minced onion | pineapple, drained |
| 40 g minced bell pepper | |

1. Shape sausage into 3 or 4 thin patties. Air fry at 200°C for 6 to 8 minutes or until well done. Remove from air fryer, drain, and crumble. Set aside. 2. Place butter, onion, and bell pepper in baking pan. Roast at 200°C for 1 minute and stir. Cook 3 to 4 minutes longer or just until vegetables are tender. 3. Add sausage, rice, and pineapple to vegetables and stir together. 4. Roast for 2 to 3 minutes, until heated through.

# Broccoli–Cheddar Twice–Baked Potatoes

**Prep time: 10 minutes | Cook time: 46 minutes |**

**Serves 4**

| | |
|---|---|
| Oil, for spraying | 1 tablespoon sour cream |
| 2 medium Maris Piper potatoes | 1 teaspoon garlic powder |
| 1 tablespoon olive oil | 1 teaspoon onion powder |
| 30 g broccoli florets | 60 g shredded Cheddar cheese |

1. Line the air fryer basket with parchment and spray lightly with oil. 2. Rinse the potatoes and pat dry with paper towels. Rub the outside of the potatoes with the olive oil and place them in the prepared basket. 3. Air fry at 200°C for 40 minutes, or until easily pierced with a fork. Let cool just enough to handle, then cut the potatoes in half lengthwise. 4. Meanwhile, place the broccoli in a microwave-safe bowl, cover with water, and microwave on high for 5 to 8 minutes. Drain and set aside. 5. Scoop out most of the potato flesh and transfer to a medium bowl. 6. Add the sour cream, garlic, and onion powder and stir until the potatoes are mashed. 7. Spoon the potato mixture back into the hollowed potato skins, mounding it to fit, if necessary. Top with the broccoli and cheese. Return the potatoes to the basket. You may need to work in batches, depending on the size of your air fryer. 8. Air fry at 200°C for 3 to 6 minutes, or until the cheese has melted. Serve immediately.

## Brussels Sprouts with Pecans and Gorgonzola

**Prep time: 10 minutes | Cook time: 25 minutes | Serves 4**

| | |
|---|---|
| 65 g pecans | Salt and freshly ground black |
| 680 g fresh Brussels sprouts, | pepper, to taste |
| trimmed and quartered | 30 g crumbled Gorgonzola |
| 2 tablespoons olive oil | cheese |

1. Spread the pecans in a single layer of the air fryer and set the heat to 180°C. Air fry for 3 to 5 minutes until the pecans are lightly browned and fragrant. Transfer the pecans to a plate and continue preheating the air fryer, increasing the heat to 200°C. 2. In a large bowl, toss the Brussels sprouts with the olive oil and season with salt and black pepper to taste. 3. Working in batches if necessary, arrange the Brussels sprouts in a single layer in the air fryer basket. Pausing halfway through the baking time to shake the basket, air fry for 20 to 25 minutes until the sprouts are tender and starting to brown on the edges. 4. Transfer the sprouts to a serving bowl and top with the toasted pecans and Gorgonzola. Serve warm or at room temperature.

## Green Peas with Mint

**Prep time: 5 minutes | Cook time: 5 minutes | Serves 4**

| | |
|---|---|
| 75 g shredded lettuce | 1 tablespoon fresh mint, |
| 1 (280 g) package frozen green | shredded |
| peas, thawed | 1 teaspoon melted butter |

1. Lay the shredded lettuce in the air fryer basket. 2. Toss together the peas, mint, and melted butter and spoon over the lettuce. 3. Air fry at 180°C for 5 minutes, until peas are warm and lettuce wilts.

## Crispy Lemon Artichoke Hearts

**Prep time: 10 minutes | Cook time: 15 minutes | Serves 2**

| | |
|---|---|
| 1 (425 g) can artichoke hearts | 30 g whole wheat bread crumbs |
| in water, drained | ¼ teaspoon salt |
| 1 egg | ¼ teaspoon paprika |
| 1 tablespoon water | ½ lemon |

1. Preheat the air fryer to 190°C. 2. In a medium shallow bowl, beat together the egg and water until frothy. 3. In a separate medium shallow bowl, mix together the bread crumbs, salt, and paprika. 4. Dip each artichoke heart into the egg mixture, then into the bread crumb mixture, coating the outside with the crumbs. Place the artichokes hearts in a single layer of the air fryer basket. 5. Fry the artichoke hearts for 15 minutes. 6. Remove the artichokes from the air fryer, and squeeze fresh lemon juice over the top before serving.

## Chiles Rellenos with Red Chile Sauce

**Prep time: 20 minutes | Cook time: 20 minutes | Serves 2**

| | |
|---|---|
| Peppers: | oil |
| 2 poblano peppers, rinsed and | 25 g finely chopped yellow |
| dried | onion |
| 110 g thawed frozen or drained | 2 teaspoons minced garlic |
| canned corn kernels | 1 (170 g) can tomato paste |
| 1 spring onion, sliced | 2 tablespoons ancho chili |
| 2 tablespoons chopped fresh | powder |
| coriander | 1 teaspoon dried oregano |
| ½ teaspoon coarse sea salt | 1 teaspoon ground cumin |
| ¼ teaspoon black pepper | ½ teaspoon coarse sea salt |
| 150 g grated Monterey Jack | 470 ml chicken stock |
| cheese | 2 tablespoons fresh lemon juice |
| Sauce: | Mexican crema or sour cream, |
| 3 tablespoons extra-virgin olive | for serving |

1. For the peppers: Place the peppers in the air fryer basket. Set the air fryer to 200°C for 10 minutes, turning the peppers halfway through the cooking time, until their skins are charred. Transfer the peppers to a resealable plastic bag, seal, and set aside to steam for 5 minutes. Peel the peppers and discard the skins. Cut a slit down the centre of each pepper, starting at the stem and continuing to the tip. Remove the seeds, being careful not to tear the chile. 2. In a medium bowl, combine the corn, spring onion, coriander, salt, black pepper, and cheese; set aside. 3. Meanwhile, for the sauce: In a large skillet, heat the olive oil over medium-high heat. Add the onion and cook, stirring, until tender, about 5 minutes. Add the garlic and cook, stirring, for 30 seconds. Stir in the tomato paste, chile powder, oregano, and cumin, and salt. Cook, stirring, for 1 minute. Whisk in the stock and lemon juice. Bring to a simmer and cook, stirring occasionally, while the stuffed peppers finish cooking. 4. Cut a slit down the centre of each poblano pepper, starting at the stem and continuing to the tip. Remove the seeds, being careful not to tear the chile. 5. Carefully stuff each pepper with half the corn mixture. Place the stuffed peppers in a baking pan. Place the pan in the air fryer basket. Set the air fryer to 200°C for 10 minutes, or until the cheese has melted. 6. Transfer the stuffed peppers to a serving platter and drizzle with the sauce and some crema.

# Buttery Green Beans

**Prep time: 5 minutes | Cook time: 8 to 10 minutes | Serves 6**

450 g green beans, trimmed

1 tablespoon avocado oil

1 teaspoon garlic powder

Sea salt and freshly ground black pepper, to taste

4 tablespoons unsalted butter, melted

20 g freshly grated Parmesan cheese

1. In a large bowl, toss together the green beans, avocado oil, and garlic powder and season with salt and pepper. 2. Set the air fryer to 200ºC. Arrange the green beans in a single layer in the air fryer basket. Air fry for 8 to 10 minutes, tossing halfway through. 3. Transfer the beans to a large bowl and toss with the melted butter. Top with the Parmesan cheese and serve warm.

# Roasted Salsa

**Prep time: 15 minutes | Cook time: 30 minutes | Makes 500 g**

2 large San Marzano tomatoes, cored and cut into large chunks

½ medium white onion, peeled and large-diced

½ medium jalapeño, seeded and large-diced

2 cloves garlic, peeled and diced

½ teaspoon salt

1 tablespoon coconut oil

65 g fresh lime juice

1. Place tomatoes, onion, and jalapeño into an ungreased round nonstick baking dish. Add garlic, then sprinkle with salt and drizzle with coconut oil. 2. Place dish into air fryer basket. Adjust the temperature to 150ºC and bake for 30 minutes. Vegetables will be dark brown around the edges and tender when done. 3. Pour mixture into a food processor or blender. Add lime juice. Process on low speed 30 seconds until only a few chunks remain. 4. Transfer salsa to a sealable container and refrigerate at least 1 hour. Serve chilled.

# Buttery Mushrooms

**Prep time: 10 minutes | Cook time: 10 minutes | Serves 4**

230 g shitake mushrooms, halved

2 tablespoons salted butter, melted

¼ teaspoon salt

¼ teaspoon ground black pepper

1. In a medium bowl, toss mushrooms with butter, then sprinkle with salt and pepper. Place into ungreased air fryer basket. Adjust the temperature to 200ºCand air fry for 10 minutes, shaking the basket halfway through cooking. Mushrooms will be tender when done. Serve warm.

# Chapter 9 Vegetarian Mains

# Chapter 9 Vegetarian Mains

## Crispy Cabbage Steaks

**Prep time: 5 minutes | Cook time: 10 minutes | Serves 4**

1 small head green cabbage, cored and cut into ½-inch-thick slices
¼ teaspoon salt
¼ teaspoon ground black pepper
2 tablespoons olive oil
1 clove garlic, peeled and finely minced
½ teaspoon dried thyme
½ teaspoon dried parsley

1. Sprinkle each side of cabbage with salt and pepper, then place into ungreased air fryer basket, working in batches if needed. 2.Drizzle each side of cabbage with olive oil, then sprinkle with remaining ingredients on both sides. 3.Adjust the temperature to 180ºC and air fry for 10 minutes, turning "steaks" halfway through cooking. 4.3.Cabbage will be browned at the edges and tender when done. 5.Serve warm.

## Spaghetti Squash Alfredo

**Prep time: 10 minutes | Cook time: 15 minutes | Serves 2**

½ large cooked spaghetti squash
2 tablespoons salted butter, melted
120 ml low-carb Alfredo sauce
60 g grated vegetarian Parmesan cheese
½ teaspoon garlic powder
1 teaspoon dried parsley
¼ teaspoon ground peppercorn
120 g shredded Italian blend cheese

1. Using a fork, remove the strands of spaghetti squash from the shell. 2.Place into a large bowl with butter and Alfredo sauce. 3.Sprinkle with Parmesan, garlic powder, parsley, and peppercorn. 4.Pour into a 1 L round baking dish and top with shredded cheese. 5.Place dish into the air fryer basket. 6.Adjust the temperature to 160ºC and bake for 15 minutes. 7.When finished, cheese will be golden and bubbling. 8.Serve immediately.

## Super Vegetable Burger

**Prep time: 15 minutes | Cook time: 12 minutes | Serves 8**

230 g cauliflower, steamed and diced, rinsed and drained
2 teaspoons coconut oil, melted
2 teaspoons minced garlic
60 g desiccated coconut
120 g oats
3 tablespoons flour
1 tablespoon flaxseeds plus 3
tablespoons water, divided
1 teaspoon mustard powder
2 teaspoons thyme
2 teaspoons parsley
2 teaspoons chives
Salt and ground black pepper, to taste
235 g breadcrumbs

1. Preheat the air fryer to 200ºC. 2.Combine the cauliflower with all the ingredients, except for the breadcrumbs, incorporating everything well. 3.Using the hands, shape 8 equal-sized amounts of the mixture into burger patties. 4.Coat the patties in breadcrumbs before putting them in the air fryer basket in a single layer. 5.Air fry for 12 minutes or until crispy. 6.Serve hot.

## Roasted Vegetable Mélange with Herbs

**Prep time: 10 minutes | Cook time: 14 to 18 minutes | Serves 4**

1 (230 g) package sliced mushrooms
1 yellow butternut squash, sliced
1 red pepper, sliced
3 cloves garlic, sliced
1 tablespoon olive oil
½ teaspoon dried basil
½ teaspoon dried thyme
½ teaspoon dried tarragon

1. Preheat the air fryer to 180ºC. 2.Toss the mushrooms, squash, and pepper with the garlic and olive oil in a large bowl until well coated. 3.Mix in the basil, thyme, and tarragon and toss again. 4.Spread the vegetables evenly in the air fryer basket and roast for 14 to 18 minutes, or until the vegetables are fork-tender. 5.Cool for 5 minutes before serving.

## Spinach–Artichoke Stuffed Mushrooms

**Prep time: 10 minutes | Cook time: 10 to 14 minutes | Serves 4**

2 tablespoons olive oil
4 large portobello mushrooms, stems removed and gills scraped out
½ teaspoon salt
¼ teaspoon freshly ground pepper
110 g goat cheese, crumbled

120 g chopped marinated artichoke hearts
235 g frozen spinach, thawed and squeezed dry
120 g grated Parmesan cheese
2 tablespoons chopped fresh parsley

1. Preheat the air fryer to 200ºC. 2.Rub the olive oil over the portobello mushrooms until thoroughly coated. 3.Sprinkle both sides with the salt and black pepper. 4.Place top-side down on a clean work surface. 5.In a small bowl, combine the goat cheese, artichoke hearts, and spinach. 6.Mash with the back of a fork until thoroughly combined. 7.Divide the cheese mixture among the mushrooms and sprinkle with the Parmesan cheese. 8.Air fry for 10 to 14 minutes until the mushrooms are tender and the cheese has begun to brown. 9.Top with the fresh parsley just before serving.

## Aubergine Parmesan

**Prep time: 15 minutes | Cook time: 17 minutes | Serves 4**

1 medium aubergine, ends trimmed, sliced into ½-inch rounds
¼ teaspoon salt
2 tablespoons coconut oil
120 g grated Parmesan cheese

30 g cheese crisps, finely crushed
120 ml low-carb marinara sauce
120 g shredded Mozzarella cheese

1. Sprinkle aubergine rounds with salt on both sides and wrap in a kitchen towel for 30 minutes. 2.Press to remove excess water, then drizzle rounds with coconut oil on both sides. 3.In a medium bowl, mix Parmesan and cheese crisps. 4.Press each aubergine slice into mixture to coat both sides. 5.Place rounds into ungreased air fryer basket. 6.Adjust the temperature to 180ºC and air fry for 15 minutes, turning rounds halfway through cooking. 7.They will be crispy around the edges when done. 8.Spoon marinara over rounds and sprinkle with Mozzarella. 9.Continue cooking an additional 2 minutes at 180ºC until cheese is melted. 10.Serve warm.

## Pesto Spinach Flatbread

**Prep time: 10 minutes | Cook time: 8 minutes | Serves 4**

235 g blanched finely ground almond flour
60 g soft white cheese
475 g shredded Mozzarella

cheese
235 g chopped fresh spinach leaves
2 tablespoons basil pesto

1. Place flour, soft white cheese, and Mozzarella in a large microwave-safe bowl and microwave on high 45 seconds, then stir. 2.Fold in spinach and microwave an additional 15 seconds. 3.Stir until a soft dough ball forms. 4.Cut two pieces of parchment paper to fit air fryer basket. 5.Separate dough into two sections and press each out on ungreased parchment to create 6-inch rounds. 6.Spread 1 tablespoon pesto over each flatbread and place rounds on parchment into ungreased air fryer basket. 7.Adjust the temperature to 180ºC and air fry for 8 minutes, turning crusts halfway through cooking. 8.Flatbread will be golden when done. 9.Let cool 5 minutes before slicing and serving.

## Herbed Broccoli with Cheese

**Prep time: 5 minutes | Cook time: 18 minutes | Serves 4**

1 large-sized head broccoli, stemmed and cut into small florets
2½ tablespoons rapeseed oil
2 teaspoons dried basil

2 teaspoons dried rosemary
Salt and ground black pepper, to taste
80 g grated yellow cheese

1. Bring a pot of lightly salted water to a boil. 2.Add the broccoli florets to the boiling water and let boil for about 3 minutes. 3.Drain the broccoli florets well and transfer to a large bowl. 4.Add the rapeseed oil, basil, rosemary, salt, and black pepper to the bowl and toss until the broccoli is fully coated. 5.Preheat the air fryer to 200ºC. 6.Place the broccoli in the air fryer basket and air fry for about 15 minutes, shaking the basket halfway through, or until the broccoli is crisp. 7.Serve the broccoli warm with grated cheese sprinkled on top.

# Courgette–Ricotta Tart

**Prep time: 15 minutes | Cook time: 60 minutes | Serves 6**

120 g grated Parmesan cheese, divided
350 g almond flour
1 tablespoon coconut flour
½ teaspoon garlic powder
¾ teaspoon salt, divided
60 g unsalted butter, melted

1 courgette, thinly sliced (about 475 ml)
235 g Ricotta cheese
3 eggs
2 tablespoons double cream
2 cloves garlic, minced
½ teaspoon dried tarragon

1. Preheat the air fryer to 170ºC. 2.Coat a round pan with olive oil and set aside. 3.In a large bowl, whisk 60 g Parmesan with the almond flour, coconut flour, garlic powder, and ¼ teaspoon of the salt. 4.Stir in the melted butter until the dough resembles coarse crumbs. 5.Press the dough firmly into the bottom and up the sides of the prepared pan. 6.Air fry for 12 to 15 minutes until the crust begins to brown. 7.Let cool to room temperature. 8.Meanwhile, place the courgette in a colander and sprinkle with the remaining ½ teaspoon salt. 9.Toss gently to distribute the salt and let sit for 30 minutes. 10.Use paper towels to pat the courgette dry. 11.In a large bowl, whisk together the ricotta, eggs, double cream, garlic, and tarragon. 12.Gently stir in the courgette slices. 13.Pour the cheese mixture into the cooled crust and sprinkle with the remaining 60 g Parmesan. 14.Increase the air fryer to 180ºC. 15.Place the pan in the air fryer basket and air fry for 45 to 50 minutes, or until set and a tester inserted into the centre of the tart comes out clean. 16.Serve warm or at room temperature.

# Super Veg Rolls

**Prep time: 20 minutes | Cook time: 10 minutes | Serves 6**

2 potatoes, mashed
60 g peas
60 g mashed carrots
1 small cabbage, sliced
60 g beans

2 tablespoons sweetcorn
1 small onion, chopped
120 g breadcrumbs
1 packet spring roll sheets
120 g cornflour slurry (mix 40 g cornflour with 80 ml water)

1. Preheat the air fryer to 200ºC. 2.Boil all the vegetables in water over a low heat. 3.Rinse and allow to dry. 4.Unroll the spring roll sheets and spoon equal amounts of vegetable onto the centre of each one. 5.Fold into spring rolls and coat each one with the slurry and breadcrumbs. 6.Air fry the rolls in the preheated air fryer for 10 minutes. 7.Serve warm.

# Chapter 10 Desserts

# Chapter 10 Desserts

## Cream Cheese Danish

**Prep time: 20 minutes | Cook time: 15 minutes | Serves 6**

| | |
|---|---|
| 35 g blanched finely ground almond flour | 2 large egg yolks |
| 225 g shredded Mozzarella cheese | 75 g powdered sweetener, divided |
| 140 g full-fat cream cheese, divided | 2 teaspoons vanilla extract, divided |

1. In a large microwave-safe bowl, add almond flour, Mozzarella, and 30 g cream cheese. Mix and then microwave for 1 minute. 2. Stir and add egg yolks to the bowl. Continue stirring until soft dough forms. Add 50 g sweetener to dough and 1 teaspoon vanilla. 3. Cut a piece of baking paper to fit your air fryer basket. Wet your hands with warm water and press out the dough into a ¼-inch-thick rectangle. 4. In a medium bowl, mix remaining cream cheese, remaining sweetener, and vanilla. Place this cream cheese mixture on the right half of the dough rectangle. Fold over the left side of the dough and press to seal. Place into the air fryer basket. 5. Adjust the temperature to 160ºC and bake for 15 minutes. 6. After 7 minutes, flip over the Danish. 7. When done, remove the Danish from baking paper and allow to completely cool before cutting.

## Brown Sugar Banana Bread

**Prep time: 20 minutes | Cook time: 22 to 24 minutes | Serves 4**

| | |
|---|---|
| 195 g packed light brown sugar | 1½ teaspoons baking powder |
| 1 large egg, beaten | 1 teaspoon ground cinnamon |
| 2 tablespoons unsalted butter, melted | ½ teaspoon salt |
| 120 ml milk, whole or semi-skimmed | 1 banana, mashed |
| 250 g All-purpose flour | 1 to 2 tablespoons coconut, or avocado oil oil |
| | 20 g icing sugar (optional) |

1. In a large bowl, stir together the brown sugar, egg, melted butter, and milk. 2. In a medium bowl, whisk the flour, baking powder, cinnamon, and salt until blended. Add the flour mixture to the sugar mixture and stir just to blend. 3. Add the mashed banana and stir to combine. 4. Preheat the air fryer to 180ºC. Spritz 2 mini loaf pans with oil. 5. Evenly divide the batter between the prepared pans and place them in the air fryer basket. 6. Cook for 22 to 24 minutes, or until a knife inserted into the middle of the loaves comes out clean. 7. Dust the warm loaves with icing sugar (if using).

## Coconut–Custard Pie

**Prep time: 10 minutes | Cook time: 20 to 23 minutes | Serves 4**

| | |
|---|---|
| 240 ml milk | 2 eggs |
| 40 g granulated sugar, plus 2 tablespoons | 2 tablespoons melted butter |
| 30 g scone mix | Cooking spray |
| 1 teaspoon vanilla extract | 50 g shredded coconut |

1. Place all ingredients except coconut in a medium bowl. 2. Using a hand mixer, beat on high speed for 3 minutes. 3. Let sit for 5 minutes. 4. Preheat the air fryer to 160ºC. 5. Spray a baking pan with cooking spray and place pan in air fryer basket. 6. Pour filling into pan and sprinkle coconut over top. 7. Cook pie for 20 to 23 minutes or until center sets.

## Gingerbread

**Prep time: 5 minutes | Cook time: 20 minutes | Makes 1 loaf**

| | |
|---|---|
| Cooking spray | ⅛ teaspoon salt |
| 65 g All-purpose flour | 1 egg |
| 2 tablespoons granulated sugar | 70 g treacle |
| ¾ teaspoon ground ginger | 120 ml buttermilk |
| ¼ teaspoon cinnamon | 2 tablespoons coconut, or avocado oil |
| 1 teaspoon baking powder | |
| ½ teaspoon baking soda | 1 teaspoon pure vanilla extract |

1. Preheat the air fryer to 160ºC. 2. Spray a baking dish lightly with cooking spray. 3. In a medium bowl, mix together all the dry ingredients. 4. In a separate bowl, beat the egg. Add treacle, buttermilk, oil, and vanilla and stir until well mixed. 5. Pour liquid mixture into dry ingredients and stir until well blended. 6. Pour batter into baking dish and bake for 20 minutes, or until toothpick inserted in center of loaf comes out clean.

# Blackberry Cobbler

**Prep time: 15 minutes | Cook time: 25 to 30 minutes | Serves 6**

| | |
|---|---|
| 330 g fresh or frozen blackberries | 1 teaspoon vanilla extract |
| 260 g granulated sugar, divided into 200 g and 150 g | 8 tablespoons butter, melted |
| | 65 g self-raising flour |
| | 1 to 2 tablespoons oil |

1. In a medium bowl, stir together the blackberries, 200 g of sugar, and vanilla. 2. In another medium bowl, stir together the melted butter, remaining 150 g of sugar, and flour until a dough forms. 3. Spritz a baking pan with oil. Add the blackberry mixture. Crumble the flour mixture over the fruit. Cover the pan with aluminum foil. 4. Preheat the air fryer to 180ºC. 5. Place the covered pan in the air fryer basket. Cook for 20 to 25 minutes until the filling is thickened. 6. Uncover the pan and cook for 5 minutes more, depending on how juicy and browned you like your cobbler. Let sit for 5 minutes before serving.

# Pumpkin Spice Pecans

**Prep time: 5 minutes | Cook time: 6 minutes | Serves 4**

| | |
|---|---|
| 125 g whole pecans | ½ teaspoon ground cinnamon |
| 50 g granulated sweetener | ½ teaspoon pumpkin pie spice |
| 1 large egg white | ½ teaspoon vanilla extract |

1. Toss all ingredients in a large bowl until pecans are coated. Place into the air fryer basket. 2. Adjust the temperature to 150ºC and air fry for 6 minutes. 3. Toss two to three times during cooking. 4. Allow to cool completely. Store in an airtight container up to 3 days.

# Applesauce and Chocolate Brownies

**Prep time: 10 minutes | Cook time: 15 minutes | Serves 8**

| | |
|---|---|
| 15 g unsweetened cocoa powder | 80 g granulated sugar |
| 15 g All-purpose flour | 1 large egg |
| ¼ teaspoon kosher, or coarse sea salt | 3 tablespoons unsweetened applesauce |
| ½ teaspoons baking powder | 50 g miniature semisweet chocolate chips |
| 3 tablespoons unsalted butter, melted | Coarse sea salt, to taste |

1. Preheat the air fryer to 150ºC. 2. In a large bowl, whisk together the cocoa powder, All-purpose flour, kosher salt, and baking powder. 3. In a separate large bowl, combine the butter, granulated sugar, egg, and applesauce, then use a spatula to fold in the cocoa powder mixture and the chocolate chips until well combined. 4. Spray a baking pan with nonstick cooking spray, then pour the mixture into the pan. Place the pan in the air fryer and bake for 15 minutes or until a toothpick comes out clean when inserted in the middle. 5. Remove the brownies from the air fryer, sprinkle some coarse sea salt on top, and allow to cool in the pan on a wire rack for 20 minutes before cutting and serving.

# Lemon Curd Pavlova

**Prep time: 10 minutes | Cook time: 1 hour | Serves 4**

| | |
|---|---|
| Shell: | 50 g powdered sweetener |
| 3 large egg whites | 120 ml lemon juice |
| ¼ teaspoon cream of tartar | 4 large eggs |
| 40 g powdered sweetener | 120 ml coconut oil |
| 1 teaspoon grated lemon zest | For Garnish (Optional): |
| 1 teaspoon lemon extract | Blueberries |
| Lemon Curd: | powdered sweetener |

1. Preheat the air fryer to 140ºC. Thoroughly grease a pie pan with butter or coconut oil. 2. Make the shell: In a small bowl, use a hand mixer to beat the egg whites and cream of tartar until soft peaks form. With the mixer on low, slowly sprinkle in the sweetener and mix until it's completely incorporated. 3. Add the lemon zest and lemon extract and continue to beat with the hand mixer until stiff peaks form. 4. Spoon the mixture into the greased pie pan, then smooth it across the bottom, up the sides, and onto the rim to form a shell. Bake for 1 hour, then turn off the air fryer and let the shell stand in the air fryer for 20 minutes. (The shell can be made up to 3 days ahead and stored in an airtight container in the refrigerator, if desired.) 5. While the shell bakes, make the lemon curd: In a medium-sized heavy-bottomed saucepan, whisk together the sweetener, lemon juice, and eggs. Add the coconut oil and place the pan on the stovetop over medium heat. Once the oil is melted, whisk constantly until the mixture thickens and thickly coats the back of a spoon, about 10 minutes. Do not allow the mixture to come to a boil. 6. Pour the lemon curd mixture through a fine-mesh strainer into a medium-sized bowl. Place the bowl inside a larger bowl filled with ice water and whisk occasionally until the curd is completely cool, about 15 minutes. 7. Place the lemon curd on top of the shell and garnish with blueberries and powdered sweetener, if desired. Store leftovers in the refrigerator for up to 4 days.

# Coconut Mixed Berry Crisp

**Prep time: 5 minutes | Cook time: 20 minutes |**
**Serves 6**

| | |
|---|---|
| 1 tablespoon butter, melted | ½ teaspoon ground cinnamon |
| 340 g mixed berries | ¼ teaspoon ground cloves |
| 65 g granulated sweetener | ¼ teaspoon grated nutmeg |
| 1 teaspoon pure vanilla extract | 50 g coconut chips, for garnish |

1. Preheat the air fryer to 160°C. Coat a baking pan with melted butter. 2. Put the remaining ingredients except the coconut chips in the prepared baking pan. 3. Bake in the preheated air fryer for 20 minutes. 4. Serve garnished with the coconut chips.

# Baked Brazilian Pineapple

**Prep time: 10 minutes | Cook time: 10 minutes |**
**Serves 4**

| | |
|---|---|
| 60 g brown sugar | cored, and cut into spears |
| 2 teaspoons ground cinnamon | 3 tablespoons unsalted butter, |
| 1 small pineapple, peeled, | melted |

1. In a small bowl, mix the brown sugar and cinnamon until thoroughly combined. 2. Brush the pineapple spears with the melted butter. Sprinkle the cinnamon-sugar over the spears, pressing lightly to ensure it adheres well. 3. Place the spears in the air fryer basket in a single layer. (Depending on the size of your air fryer, you may have to do this in batches.) Set the air fryer to 200°C and cook for 10 minutes for the first batch (6 to 8 minutes for the next batch, as the fryer will be preheated). Halfway through the cooking time, brush the spears with butter. 4. The pineapple spears are done when they are heated through, and the sugar is bubbling. Serve hot.

# Peaches and Apple Crumble

**Prep time: 10 minutes | Cook time: 10 to 12 minutes**
**| Serves 4**

| | |
|---|---|
| 2 peaches, peeled, pitted, and chopped | All-purpose flour |
| 1 apple, peeled and chopped | 2 tablespoons unsalted butter, at room temperature |
| 2 tablespoons honey | 3 tablespoons packed brown |
| 45 g quick-cooking oats | sugar |
| 25 g whole-wheat pastry, or | ½ teaspoon ground cinnamon |

1. Preheat the air fryer to 190°C. 2. Mix together the peaches, apple, and honey in a baking pan until well incorporated. 3. In a bowl, combine the oats, pastry flour, butter, brown sugar, and cinnamon and stir to mix well. Spread this mixture evenly over the fruit. 4. Place the baking pan in the air fryer basket and bake for 10 to 12 minutes, or until the fruit is bubbling around the edges and the topping is golden brown. 5. Remove from the basket and serve warm.

# Pears with Honey–Lemon Ricotta

**Prep time: 10 minutes | Cook time: 8 minutes |**
**Serves 4**

| | |
|---|---|
| 2 large Bartlett pears | 125 g full-fat ricotta cheese |
| 3 tablespoons butter, melted | 1 tablespoon honey, plus |
| 3 tablespoons brown sugar | additional for drizzling |
| ½ teaspoon ground ginger | 1 teaspoon pure almond extract |
| ¼ teaspoon ground cardamom | 1 teaspoon pure lemon extract |

1. Peel each pear and cut in half, lengthwise. Use a melon baller to scoop out the core. Place the pear halves in a medium bowl, add the melted butter, and toss. Add the brown sugar, ginger, and cardamom; toss to coat. 2. Place the pear halves, cut side down, in the air fryer basket. Set the air fryer to 190°C cooking for 8 to 10 minutes, or until the pears are lightly browned and tender, but not mushy. 3. Meanwhile, in a medium bowl, combine the ricotta, honey, and almond and lemon extracts. Beat with an electric mixer on medium speed until the mixture is light and fluffy, about 1 minute. 4. To serve, divide the ricotta mixture among four small shallow bowls. Place a pear half, cut side up, on top of the cheese. Drizzle with additional honey and serve.

# Peanut Butter, Honey & Banana Toast

**Prep time: 10 minutes | Cook time: 9 minutes |**
**Serves 4**

| | |
|---|---|
| 2 tablespoons unsalted butter, softened | 2 bananas, peeled and thinly sliced |
| 4 slices white bread | 4 tablespoons honey |
| 4 tablespoons peanut butter | 1 teaspoon ground cinnamon |

1. Spread butter on one side of each slice of bread, then peanut butter on the other side. Arrange the banana slices on top of the peanut butter sides of each slice (about 9 slices per toast). Drizzle honey on top of the banana and sprinkle with cinnamon. 2. Cut each slice in half lengthwise so that it will better fit into the air fryer basket. Arrange two pieces of bread, butter sides down, in the air fryer basket. Set the air fryer to 190°C cooking for 5 minutes. Then set the air fryer to 200°C and cook for an additional 4 minutes, or until the bananas have started to brown. Repeat with remaining slices. Serve hot.

# Cherry Pie

**Prep time: 15 minutes | Cook time: 35 minutes | Serves 6**

All-purpose flour, for dusting
1 package of shortcrust pastry, cut in half, at room temperature
350 g can cherry pie filling

1 egg
1 tablespoon water
1 tablespoon sugar

1. Dust a work surface with flour and place the piecrust on it. Roll out the piecrust. Invert a shallow air fryer baking pan, or your own pie pan that fits inside the air fryer basket, on top of the dough. Trim the dough around the pan, making your cut ½ inch wider than the pan itself. 2. Repeat with the second piecrust but make the cut the same size as or slightly smaller than the pan. 3. Put the larger crust in the bottom of the baking pan. Don't stretch the dough. Gently press it into the pan. 4. Spoon in enough cherry pie filling to fill the crust. Do not overfill. 5. Using a knife or pizza cutter, cut the second piecrust into 1-inch-wide strips. Weave the strips in a lattice pattern over the top of the cherry pie filling. 6. Insert the crisper plate into the basket and the basket into the unit. Preheat to 160ºC. 7. In a small bowl, whisk the egg and water. Gently brush the egg wash over the top of the pie. Sprinkle with the sugar and cover the pie with aluminum foil. 8. Once the unit is preheated, place the pie into the basket. 9. Bake for 30 minutes, remove the foil and resume cooking for 3 to 5 minutes more. The finished pie should have a flaky golden-brown crust and bubbling pie filling. 10. When the cooking is complete, serve warm. Refrigerate leftovers for a few days.

# Grilled Peaches

**Prep time: 5 minutes | Cook time: 10 minutes | Serves 4**

Coconut, or avocado oil, for spraying
25 g crushed digestive biscuits
40 g packed light brown sugar
8 tablespoons unsalted butter

¼ teaspoon cinnamon
2 peaches, pitted and cut into quarters
4 scoops vanilla ice cream

1. Line the air fryer basket with baking paper, and spray lightly with oil. 2. In a small bowl, mix together the crushed biscuits, brown sugar, butter, and cinnamon with a fork until crumbly. 3. Place the peach wedges in the prepared basket, skin-side up. You may need to work in batches, depending on the size of your air fryer. 4. Air fry at 180ºC for 5 minutes, flip, and sprinkle with a spoonful of the biscuit mixture. Cook for another 5 minutes, or until tender and caramelized. 5. Top with a scoop of vanilla ice cream and any remaining crumble mixture. Serve immediately.

Printed in Great Britain
by Amazon